Also by Joanne M. Friedman:

It's a Horse's Life!
(Advice and Observations for the Humans Who Choose to Share It)

Horses in the Yard
(and Other Equestrian Dilemmas)

Horses Happen!
(A Survival Guide for First-Time Horse Owners)

HORSE BOUND

THE VIEW FROM THE TOP OF MOUNT MANURE

JOANNE M. FRIEDMAN

iUniverse LLC
Bloomington

iUniverse books may be ordered through booksellers or by contacting:

iUniverse
1663 Liberty Drive
Bloomington, IN 47403
www.iuniverse.com
1-800-Authors (1-800-288-4677)

Because of the dynamic nature of the Internet, any web addresses or links contained in this book may have changed since publication and may no longer be valid. The views expressed in this work are solely those of the author and do not necessarily reflect the views of the publisher, and the publisher hereby disclaims any responsibility for them.

Any people depicted in stock imagery provided by Thinkstock are models, and such images are being used for illustrative purposes only. Certain stock imagery © Thinkstock.

ISBN: 978-1-4917-0844-6 (sc)
ISBN: 978-1-4917-0845-3 (e)

Library of Congress Control Number: 2013916860

Printed in the United States of America.

iUniverse rev. date: 10/28/2013

With much love and gratitude to the horses,
friends, and family members who make
it possible for me to be an old horsewoman.

CONTENTS

INTRODUCTION

Once upon a time, I was a perfectly normal high school special education teacher. I had classes and students and goals and lesson plans, and all was right with the world. I was a horsewoman, but it was something just for my free time and an easy way to pick up extra cash when I needed it (and what horse owner doesn't need it?) mucking stalls and giving lessons.

In 1997 I lost my mind and bought Gallant Hope Farm. Since then, the place morphed from lesson and training barn to boarding farm to my own private bastion against the larger horse world. Now it's just me and my personal horses with a single boarder who has been here since the first December we were on this place. By the time I retired from teaching school, I was ready for a major change in my life. I had horses. Lord knows I had horses! But not like this. Not in my backyard every day … and every night. The horses are my sickness, my sanity, and my source of humor.

For instance, my big paint gelding, Zips Memory (a.k.a. Zips Money Pit, Doodlebug, and Get Off My Damn Foot!), was definitely giving me the stink eye this morning. I swear I saw it. He heard the vet's truck pull up and turned that evil eye on me, the one that says, "Oh, you *think* so, do you?" Naturally I allowed sanity to reign and opted to start the spring shots from the far end of the barn, with Zip up last. My vet is energetic, solid, and younger than I, with lots of experience with racehorses and such, and he learned long ago that my Zip holds no truck with the blue jumpsuits that many vets have adopted as safe-and-easy work attire. Zip can spot a jumpsuit at fifty yards. On this day, as the vet unfurled his lanky, shirt-sleeved frame from the truck's cab, I reminded Zip that this is a fine thing to do on a sunny day and waved a handful of remorse-cookies under his nose.

While the vet and I went from stall to stall, talking politics, removing the horses' blankets (I shoot them up early for all of the mosquito-borne diseases, so it was March and chilly as heck) for their annual school pictures for their Coggins tests (for equine infectious anemia), and sticking them as we went, Zip regaled us with an assortment of tricks. My vet, his racetrack experience a fine teacher of patience, is an ace at ignoring Zip, which invariably results in escalation of effort on the gelding's part. There was the stretching his front legs out under the stall guard (always makes the reserved and otherwise eloquent vet give a startled exclamatory grunt—"*Uh!*"—which is Zip's version of an Oscar). That rolled into the slamming shut of the miniature horse's stall door, which is just within reach of Zip's outstretched head, and the scratching of Zip's mega butt on the stall guard till the vinyl panel looked like it was going to burst under the strain.

The performance was capped by the pièce de résistance move of slamming the mini's stall door shut just as I tried to convince the little guy it was safe to go back inside for reblanketing. The fun never stops on Zip's watch.

Most people would probably have just thrown the needle at the big guy from across the barn aisle and called it done, but my awesomely patient vet and I have been working around Zip's frizzy brain hair for some sixteen years, long enough to know that, when stomp comes to buck, he's going to be the best behaved of the herd—as long as the barn doors are closed. I'm confident, not stupid. An open door is sufficient invitation for a spin-and-romp up and down the aisle and in and out of the barn, greet-threatening the other horses one by one, dropping important stuff in the water bucket, and creating general unrest among the natives until boredom sets in and Zip parks himself in the crossties to await the obeisance of his minions—us. So, doors closed, Zip shook off his alter ego and strode from his lair to pose for the camera like the rock star he is—left side, right side, head-on—and stood without flinching for the shots and blood draw. Go figure, right?

The process got me thinking about how many of us must be living with horses that make us want to pull our hair out. These are the ones that perturb us so badly that we find ourselves hiding behind the bedroom curtains, staring at them through the window and wondering how in hell we wound up in this predicament and whether a quick call to the local police might be in order.

Me: Uh, can you send a car over here, pronto?

State Trooper Dispatch: What's the problem, ma'am? Bear attack? Intruder? Trespasser? Horse giving you the stink eye again?

They know me at the State Police barracks, and I'd bet my number on the caller ID is enough to make them run a real quick survey on which newbie cop might be around who needs a good laugh. They can't hide from me, but they don't have to join hands with my lunacy.

Thinking about it led to writing about it, and suddenly another book appeared to partner with *It's a Horse's Life!*, *Horses in the Yard*, and *Horses Happen!* This collection of brand-new essays tracing the exploits of the horses of Gallant Hope Farm and my thoughts on the subject, therefore, is for all horse-bound humans who are old enough to know better and have ever had, currently have, or probably will have a horse that drives them crazy. I've had my share. There was the paint mare, pregnant and foundered and right off the track. And there was the "gift horse" thoroughbred mare that was recently regifted to me. And of course, there's the ever-popular "husband horse," meant for my significant other but naturally winding up mine. If you have more than one such horse, *Horse Bound: The View from the Top of Mount Manure* is probably not enough medicine to make it all go away, so add gin and stir with ice. You won't be able to read, but you won't care.

Joanne (a.k.a. Zips's Mom 2)

New girl in town! Zip is smitten. Dolly is playing it cool.

CHAPTER I

THE ODD DUCK

Between us, over a period of roughly thirty years, my daughter, Jessica, and I have owned and operated fifteen horses and one horse farm, Gallant Hope Farm in Hampton Township, New Jersey. I've been involved with horses for more than fifty years, long enough to know better. I've ridden them, trained them, worked at boarding farms, and boarded horses at my own place. Far wiser than her older mother, Jess left some years ago for greener pastures, giving my personal crazy plenty of space and time to blossom. She, her husband, and their kids have one dog and two horses (soon to be one, as the thoroughbred mare, Dolly, will be coming home to trot on my farm and, I assume, resume her personal busy-ness of circling the horses in the pasture and driving them from one section to another for no apparent reason).

That's not strictly accurate. Dolly always has a reason. An animal communicator (pet psychic) once did a telephone reading on the Doll Baby (I was on the phone, not the horse). The way it works is you (human) call a number. A voice on the other end asks for some identifying points about the horse (sex, age, color) so it can be located in space. Then you (human) listen in while she (communicator) engages the equine (horse) in conversation. In fact, Dolly was not the original target of the psychic analysis, but the voice on the phone insisted that the problem I'd called about had her as the source. The horses had stopped allowing me to approach them in the pasture, a situation completely unacceptable and incomprehensible, given that these had been my horses for several years.

The communicator explained that the mare lives at the crossroads of utter paranoia and learning disability. To wit:

Me: So what's up with Dolly rounding up the herd and driving them to the farthest pasture?

Psychic: Things confuse Dolly. She's easily thrown off. She thinks she understands something, and then the smallest thing throws her off. She was watching a red-tailed hawk chasing something, and it made her start to worry about the sky. She's worried about things coming from the sky. What if there are birds bigger than that bird?

Me: Ah! So she's worried about flying, horse-eating monsters! That makes sense in some universe, I'm sure. Can she stop running backward over the judge at shows?

Psychic: She says she owns the problem. She knows she gets easily spooked at that point in time … Dolly will try not to be scared. You need to meditate with Dolly.

Me: [silence]

It was ever thus and ever shall be. Dollytown is a lovely place to visit as long as your nerves are strong and your coffee stronger. The nice thing about horses is that they live outside, so there are endless possibilities for separating oneself from the chain of events that's causing them to engage in behaviors that bring you either laughter or tears, depending on the state of your medication. Dolly's reason for moving the herd unexpectedly had to do with hawks killing rabbits and sunshine and green grass and dinosaurs and snake pits and pygmies with poisoned darts—oh my!

Though as I write this her return is still months away, I'm preparing for the challenge by checking and replacing fence posts and stocking up on calming herbs for everyone in her sphere of influence, horse and human. From here, Dolly moved out of the state (of New Jersey and of paranoia, apparently), and my daughter had great success showing her in dressage and jumping in the insane second cousin to both called "eventing." She may have matured into an amazingly brave event horse, but one doesn't unkink spiritual wiring so easily.

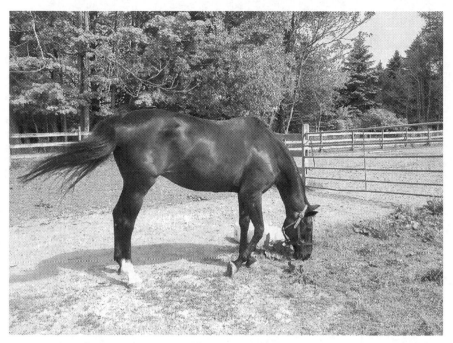

Homecoming.

My memories of Baby Doll include such signature moments as the *crack!* of the fence post she snapped during her *That gate is going to close, and I'm going to be stuck on this side forever!* phase. She was forced by unseen spirits to run hell-bent and without warning through any gate in the process of being closed, even if she had just gone through in the opposite direction. That she survived that stage of her maturational efforts was surprising. I expected at any time to find her impaled, bent, broken, and ready for permanent sleep, but that never happened. Instead, she moved on from her gate fetish to other passions, and the herd's world shifted with her.

Her fears included her truly intriguing concern over the metal strip at the back entrance to my stock trailer, which she would sniff and glare at and stare down, but which she refused to cross on certain days. She'd been around a bit and had been in that specific mode of conveyance, so there was no foreshadowing of land mines ahead.

It was a show day around 1998. Jess had her mare polished to a dapply glisten that only a dark bay can muster, and her mane and tail were neatly braided. That Jess's frustration with Dolly's inability to stand still for the very last braid at the top of her neck had caused her to burst into tears and bite the mare on the ear, at the time a little startling, is something we can laugh about now. But the job was done, and the mare looked amazing right to the moment when she had to load into the trailer.

Dolly: What the hell is that?

Jess: It's nothing. Just step over it.

Dolly: Are you kidding me? That's got to be six feet wide and ten feet tall, and it's going to break my leg and strip me of my very lifeblood if I go near it!

Jess: [sighing] Seriously? You've been in there before. You step over worse stuff getting into your stall. Stop smelling it and get on the trailer!

About thirty minutes later, Dolly was, indeed, on the trailer. *On the trailer … off the trailer … on the trailer … off the trailer.* And ten minutes after that, she was back in the pasture, braids askew, and everyone retired for the day wondering what, if anything, would have happened at the showgrounds had Dolly decided she couldn't cross the line in one direction or the other and wound up either living on the trailer or at the fairgrounds for the rest of her life. That was a question Jess opted out of answering.

Of course, the next time Dolly had to get on the trailer, she was perfect, with not a hint of histrionics, and she went on to a stellar local show and clinic career, spent six weeks in New York State at a trainer-training program, and has recently learned that Jess's brand-new Brenderup trailer needed only a few quick snorts to convince it not to eat her alive. Dolly is twenty-one. We humans aged considerably more quickly. Whether any of us matured is up for debate.

Dolly was a gift horse, by the way. She was the classic gift horse. She'd been given away at the age of three by her original owner, who couldn't quite get a handle on her training quirks. Her next owner had her for two years before he realized she wasn't serving a purpose other than feed-processing, and at five she landed in Jess's life with great fanfare. Dolly was a girl who needed her personal space. She had a mental line drawn in the sand and would, without warning, let a herd mate know when it had been crossed, even to the point of self-injury, as in her attempt to kick a horse in a neighboring paddock over the separating fence. The result of that attempt was:

Fence: 1

Dolly: 0

But for whatever reason, that line never seemed to hold at shows, whether local club affairs or cross-country events or even the Regional Irish Sport Horse Finals (no, she was neither Irish nor in any way involved in the group), which she won handily. There she would stand waiting her turn, on or off the trailer, for minutes or hours as necessary, without so much as a head toss. She is remarkable in her lack of transparency. I don't get that horse at all, and in a few weeks, she'll be mine again, in partial retirement to be my plaything. Buy your child a horse, and one day you'll find it on your doorstep, hopefully before it's too old and in need of end-of-life ministrations.

Fortunately, like so many oddly-wired horses, she's surprisingly easy to be around. She'll never be elected herd leader. It will always be an undemocratic state, with Dolly ruling by default. But from the ground and the saddle, humans never seem to have a problem with her. She was born to be owned. Now, with my daughter out of the picture, I'm waiting to see if I was born to own her.

CHAPTER 2

Ω

PONIES AND THE PEOPLE WHO HARBOR THEM

I have long subscribed to the theory that if a child is ready to ride, a full-size horse is the best option. I had some pony experiences along the way that bought me this belief. There's just something about ponies that makes them essentially different from their larger relatives, and when experience gave way to "Awwww ... but he's so *cute!*" the first of these tiny titans came through my barnyard gate.

Before you get your ire rankling, I assure you I am in no way anti-pony. They are amazing creatures and about as sturdy, willing, and useful as, say, Zip. That pretty much says it all.

I had my first close pony encounter at a boarding farm where I worked in the mid-1990s, where some fifty-plus horses were turned out together in a large pasture. The pony was great fun to be around and to play with, and I got an inkling as to how different a pony's attitude is when I watched Peanut run through the herd, pinching, tickling, nipping, and generally annoying the big horses until he roused them to chase him. At that point he'd run hell-bent for the jerry-rigged riding ring "gate"—a board that rested at half-fence height and could be lifted to allow horses to enter. Peanut was just small enough to duck under that board, and so he did, leaving a bunch of irate horses huffing and puffing on the other side while he laughed. This entertainment was free and never-ending, and we humans all enjoyed it tremendously, even if the horses weren't so thrilled.

The next pony experience, at a boarding farm where we boarders were trying hard to keep our horses alive despite the best efforts of the farm owners to kill them, was far less pleasant but still memorable. The pony in question, whose name I don't recall (blocked from memory like the pain of childbirth) was a mare, cute as a bug, who I thought liked me. This was a pasture setting with most of the equines turned out together, so retrieving any one of them meant interacting with several along the route.

This pony mare, who I'll call Cranky Butt, had historically been pleasant toward me. She was always the first to greet me on my way through the field, and she earned a chin scratch and some cooing in return. Her owners did mention something about her being a little … uh … witchy from time to time, but I hadn't seen that. Days, weeks, months went by without my seeing anything untoward from the little horse.

And then I did.

One lovely summer day as I walked out to get my mare, Cranky Butt seemed a tad out of sorts. Instead of her usual effusive greeting, she stood off a few feet and glared at me. I said hello, waved, smiled, and walked on. I don't remember now what tipped me off. Most likely it was a shout from another boarder, probably my daughter, but I turned in time to see that I was in line to be harpooned by a mouthful of very sharp teeth. I swung on her with the halter I was holding, and she wisely opted to redirect her hostility toward a nearby horse. I chalked it up to time-of-the-month blues, but there was never a safe transit through that pasture again. Until we moved to another farm, that pony mare kept one eye on me, and I could swear I could hear her brain cells frying.

Still, that's not necessarily indicative of pony-ness. Where the ponies-only aspect enters the picture is the cuteness factor. A big horse might be charming, beautiful, or elegant, and totally insane, but ponies are just so darned *cute* that it's hard to ascribe evil intent to them until it's too late. One wants to pick them up and cuddle them. One assumes that they are as sweet on the inside as they are adorable on the outside.

That's where one comes in contact with reality. A horse is a horse no matter how cute the package.

About ten years passed before the next pony happened to us. We'd given up boarding and had bought the farm (in every sense of the term). Jim Dandy was, just as his name suggests, a dandy little fellow. Jess was in need of a small schooling horse for the small schooling children, and he was just the ticket. JD was a pretty bay, part-Arab, with huge, melt-away chocolate eyes. A nicer guy would be hard to find.

JD wasn't exactly abused before Jess bought him, but close enough. He'd been a loyal show pony for a child who had outgrown him. He'd won lots of ribbons at local schooling shows. When Mommy and Daddy bought their daughter a new, full-size horse, the boarding farm owner requested that they leave JD with her to serve summer-camp duty while they moved with their new horse to a fancier barn.

By the time they decided to check on him, he was a mess. His ribs stuck out, his hide was chewed up where he'd been attacked by other horses, and a cut on his leg was growing an unlovely cauliflower of proud flesh. Still, he was as kind and accepting as could be, and we were in love. We didn't find out for another couple of weeks—when the dentist came for annual inspection and to file down pointy points, a process known, oddly, as "floating"—that the poor boy had a wolf tooth just hanging in his gum. The dentist flicked it out with his thumb. How painful that must have been boggles the mind, and that at twelve this pony had obviously never been seen by a dentist or had his teeth checked by a vet was about as odd as anything I'd seen to that point. Things got odder later, but that was an eye-opener.

The little guy did a fine job of packing on pounds and packing around my daughter's beginner riding students, but there was a tiny glitch. Jess was the one who dubbed the place where he resided "JD Land." He was a very good boy, but every now and then, without obvi-ous provocation, he would retire, mid-trot, to JD Land, where "Here Be Monsters" was on a plaque above the gate. From the outside it looked as if he'd fallen asleep under saddle, just as quiet and calm as could be. Then he'd wake up with a pronounced startle and fly halfway across the arena. There was no predicting when that would happen, no precursors of any kind, so there were a few unplanned dismounts that left a few seven-year-olds sitting in the dust wondering where the pony had gone.

Still, he was so amazingly cute that he stuck around for a couple of years until there were no advanced-beginner riders left who were small enough to ride without crushing him and no beginner-beginners balanced enough to ride his surprisingly weird canter depart. Jess handpicked his new owner from several candidates, and off he went to be loved on by a nearby grandmother and her grandbabies.

The cool thing about the JD process was that as much as we were attached to him and he worked with us in pleasant cooperation, he made it clear that any child under the age of six who wanted him was a fine owner with whom he'd leave as soon as we handed over his lead rope. While adults received barely a glance, every small child was treated to nuzzles and kisses and a sappy face that just yelled, "Take me home with you!" I never saw a horse that turned traitor so quickly and with such enthusiasm. There's a saying that every pony deserves to be owned by a little girl. JD may have written that. He certainly believed it.

No ponies here!

CHAPTER 3

SMALLEST PACKAGE, BIGGEST IRONY

Duke is anything but a pony. He's a miniature horse, period. He's also a mystical being who can morph at will, but I won't get into his spiritual aberrations.

What Duke's thirty-four and a half inches of dominance brings to the table is comic relief and endless planning. Nothing happens in the barnyard or the pasture without some thought being given to what Duke will do during the event. That he came here as a stallion is part of the problem. After seven months of happy herd life, Duke and Zip got into a tiff one day, and the world stood on end. Zip is sixteen hands of muscle. Duke is thirty-four inches of attitude. Attitude trumps muscle, and Duke had Zip pinned to the pasture fence before I could get to the gate.

Time has passed—nearly seven years since Duke landed and six since he was gelded—and we've got a routine that keeps everyone, horse and human alike, happy and safe, but there is always that heart-fluttering moment when someone accidentally goes off track and Duke becomes a force to contend with.

He's a creature of habit. Duke learns routines quickly, but not without some hysteria that goes like this:

Me: Okay, Sweet Pea, I need you to stand over in this pen for a minute while I fix your water bucket.

Duke: You *what?* Where? Here? Right here, or over here a little? Are you absolutely sure? I could die here, you know. Has anyone checked for bears or pygmies with poisoned arrows? *How can I trust you when you don't follow the rules?*

Me: It's only five feet from your regular spot.

Duke: Okay, but I'm going to have to run laps now until you put me where I belong. And I might have to try to climb the fence. I'm not making any promises.

Me: [sigh] Okay. I'm done. You can come back in now.

Duke: Whew! That was a close one. Can I have a cookie?

Once learned, a routine becomes the law of the land, and changing it in even the smallest way requires several days of preparation and several more days for adjustment. A new gate on his stall, for instance, meant two weeks of my sitting in his stall at one end of the lead while he stood planted in the aisle at the other. Cookies, cajoling, begging, pleading, cursing, click-treating every time he even thought about taking a step closer, yanking and throwing him off-balance so he'd accidentally fall into the stall, and total failure filled those two weeks in twice-daily episodes. He would walk happily into any other stall in the barn, just not that one with that mini-averse gate.

At the end of two weeks, the trauma was forgotten, and all was well. Then I changed his water bucket. A new salt block sent him quivering to the corner. The audible bird deterrent cost big bucks and two weeks of not being able to leave the farm at mealtimes as extra hands were necessary to get him into his stall. Leaving two horses in their stalls instead of one as I led him out to his pen was cause for major consternation. Just try walking him out the front door instead of the back when he's decided the back door is *his* door, and it's a festival of anxiety capped with a clicker-training session despite the fact that he's been walking out the front door for seven years.

We're still working through whatever happened in the front paddock one summer's day that scared him enough to make him unwilling to walk down the driveway with me for more than six months. This is the guy who'd been my dog-in-horse-clothing, taking long, butt-busting walks down the road every good-weather day for years. He even did it wearing a Santa hat, and I bought tiny panniers so that we could carry our own snacks should we be so inclined. It's taken me a year to get him to go as far as the mailbox—five hundred feet—and that was quite an event!

I discovered his panicky state in the way I discover so many of Duke's interesting life choices. I lay prostrate on the road; the lead thankfully self-dallied around a small tree while he tried to make a run for it back to the barn through a neighbor's yard. It seems to be related to motorcycles. That's about all I've got so far.

But on a day-to-day, minute-to-minute basis, he's truly a joy to have around. He's a huggie-bear for little kids, but he objects to hugging from adults. He stands without moving a muscle for saddling, harnessing, and trying on hats. He does tricks that he's learned in most cases in a single trial. His bow is to die for. He can be loose in the barn and "help" with the stall mucking by checking every inch for dropped grain and will exit a stall on a single command without argument. He will follow anyone who talks to him, and he'll wait patiently without a lead or tie on him while he is clipped or groomed, has his sheath cleaned, or gets his feet done or his vaccines administered. Safe as can be for toddlers and stupid adults alike, he never gives me a moment of worry that he might remove someone's body part when I'm not looking. Personable in the extreme, that's my Duke. Just never turn a blind eye toward him, and everything will be just fine. Don't assume anything; you'll make an "ass" out of "u" and "me," and you'd better have the EMS on speed dial.

Husband horse.

CHAPTER 4

The Shopping Spree

When Jess left the farm dragging her two best horses with her, we wound up short an all-purpose, do-anything-for-anyone mount that my significant other, Cliff, could hop on without having to concede that he couldn't ride worth beans. So a shopping trip ensued. We'd (and by "we" I mean "I") looked at probably a dozen horses before I came across the ad for the big-butted Appaloosa gelding. The photo was adorable. There stood Dakota, a chestnut-blanket Appaloosa with his head lowered, and at the other end of his lead was a little girl of about ten. She smiled. He seemed content. It was idyllic.

Naturally, the reality wasn't quite as peaceful as the photo. If you've never horse-shopped, you will have to trust me when I say reality is often divorced from the experience until the last possible moment, when they reconcile with a great flourish and possibly a trip to the ER. I hand it to Dakota for standing perfectly still in the ties while his owner brushed him and tacked him up for my trial ride. On this one, I hadn't bothered to bring Cliff along. I'd found out early in the shopping process that Cliff was going to defer to me no matter what he thought, and having him beside me meant I had to risk letting him fall in love with something I might not otherwise have approved of. He's a dairyman, stolid, quiet, and iconically plaid-shirted. Anything equine is labeled "Not Cow" and lumped together. His deference was not to my superior understanding and horse-whisperer-like ability to ferret out likely mounts. No, it was more on the lines of not really wanting to be bothered with the details. Hand him a horse, and he'd be good to go. Ask him to choose one, and it could become his life's work.

This was supposed to be Cliff's horse. A few weeks earlier, my daughter, Jess, had moved away, taking two of her three horses with her. The Morgan, Rat, was the everyone horse. Everyone rode him. Everyone loved him. Everyone went nuts when he left, Cliff in particular.

"*She's taking Rat?*" Cliff whimpered. "I thought he was staying here! Now what am I going to ride?"

"You don't ride," I reminded him. "You only rode him a couple of times last year."

Cliff sighed with a hangdog expression. "But what if I want to ride? What am I going to ride then? … I guess I won't be riding anymore … [sigh]."

"Good grief! Okay. If I find you a horse, will you promise to ride more than once a year?"

Cliff wriggled like a puppy. "Of course! Sure! I'll ride all the time, I promise!"

Yeah, well … that was the same lie I got from Jess when she promised to take care of the new hamster when she was four. One would think learning would have transpired.

At any rate, there I stood facing a truly lovely Appy, with "Western Pleasure" in his ad and written all over his monstrous hindquarters. Lot of quarter horse in that back end! I'd guess at least three depending on the viewing angle. I watched the barn owner take a quick ride around the ring, and then convinced I wasn't going to get killed, I hopped aboard. There was a small glitch. There was no *on* button. Much leg-thumping ensued, and finally Dakota walked off, moved grudgingly into a trot, and thought briefly about a lope before we both got tired and decided we could rest for a bit. Perfect husband horse!

The owner had told me that her hubby was the only one riding Dakota at that point. Her daughter had lost interest in the "western stuff," so the horse was only getting out about every other week on a trail ride. He hadn't damaged Hubby given the rare nonrider riding experiences, which seemed a good selling point. I urged the horse into motion, discovered he had a grudge against one corner of the ring and a really big spook to go with it, got him past that with minimal hysteria, and left a deposit check.

The next night I drove Cliff past the barn and pointed to the Appy in the pasture. I asked what he thought about this as his new horse, and he nodded. Two days later, I plunked down the rest of the cash, and Dakota was ours. Actually, he was mine, but I didn't know that just then.

I'm an owner to whom horses just happen, so shopping was a novelty for me. To say we'd looked at some "interesting" horses prior to my *big find* would be putting it mildly. It was impressive how little owners knew about their horses ... and riding, training, tacking, maintenance, body parts, and the like. One horse we looked at was advertised as a dun gelding with a dorsal stripe. He turned out to be a bay. I would have pressed the owner on the subject, but watching him tie, groom, and tack the animal suggested any answers beyond repeating his own name would have proven inconclusive. Many of the horses were actually very nice. All but one or two would have required some serious training. At least one gave me the impression that he tolerated his current owner as part of a silent nonaggression pact but that no one else would be welcome to touch him.

I did kind of regret passing up the blue-eyed, bald-faced paint mare. Her bad feet might have been redeemable, and she was lovely about letting me, a total stranger, hop aboard and take her out on the trail, including water obstacles and rocky outcrops that had to be negotiated. But the photo of that one got an immediate thumbs-down from Cliff. He didn't like her face. Her blue eyes were "spooky." If I'd been smart, I'd have photoshopped it.

And there was a handsome quarter horse I really liked, despite his special shoes (what is it with bad feet and sale horses?). I took a day to think about it. I talked to my shoer about the hoof issue. Then I called and left a message for the owner that I'd be over with the cash and the trailer at her convenience. That was the last I heard.

So Dakota it was, almost by default.

He's proved to be a nice horse. It only took him two years to accept me fully, which seemed in keeping with his generalized resistance to forward movement. He's nothing if not cautious. Our first trail ride with Cliff aboard Dakota and me on my quarter horse, Leo, was a harbinger of things to come. One thing it harbingered was that Cliff really needed to have a few lessons. There were no problems with Dakota. Cliff, on the other hand …

We made it from the riding ring to the back field—some thousand feet—without incident, Dakota occasionally picking up a jog to keep up with speedy-boy Leo, and everyone was having a fine time. Then there arose the helmet issue. I'd insisted on a helmet for Cliff, and he was about as resistant to the concept as a kid would be to spinach ice cream. By the time we'd gone a thousand feet, Cliff was complaining about the fit of my helmet on his head. I suggested he take it off and adjust the strap.

"How am I going to do that," he sniped, "when I'm on a horse?"

"Drop the reins," I suggested, "and take the damn helmet off. The horse isn't going anywhere." Of that I was entirely certain.

This was one of the first times Dakota's lack of enthusiasm really paid off, as he stood perfectly still while Cliff grumbled through strap adjustments. In a few minutes, we were back on track and headed up into the woods.

Now, keep in mind that Cliff and Dakota were behind me, and I was focused on navigating through the trees and over the rocks that comprise the "appurtenant woodlands" of my property, so it's really not surprising that I didn't see what had happened till we were back at the barnyard gate and I'd dismounted. I turned around, and there stood Dakota, his one-eared headstall now a no-eared headstall, as it had slipped off his head and was hanging below his chin. He was bravely holding the bit in his mouth.

Cliff didn't seem to have noticed.

"Do me a favor," I quietly suggested, "and get off the horse. Quickly, please."

He did as recommended and looked at me with a *what's-your-point?* expression.

"Well, the fact that the horse isn't wearing a bridle is a good start," I said. "Any idea when it might have fallen off?"

"Sure!" he chirped. "It happened as soon as we went into the woods." He smiled, looking pleased with his attention to detail.

And why wasn't I notified? Well, Cliff thought it was *supposed* to do that—some sort of cowboy thing, he said—so he didn't think it was important.

Good horses are hard to come by. Horses that will chaperone a nonrider and carry their own bit to boot are priceless. Cliff hasn't done much riding since then, but 'Kota and I are buds. I taught him that speed is fun. He taught me that rapid-fire exercises like barrel racing and pole bending might be less elegant when the horse is built like a steer, but no less exciting. I didn't think I needed another horse for myself. I guess I was wrong.

CHAPTER 5

PARANOIA STRIKES DEEP

It was a really bad couple of years for barn fires back around 2010. Several barns nearby burned down at a cost of tens of thousands of dollars in buildings and equipment and more equine lives than I care to think about. As a result, we hadn't been on vacation for a long time.

Paranoia overtook my common sense sometime after the third and before the fourth barn burned. It wasn't about the conspiracy theories that were rampant among my fellow horse-property owners. I may be obnoxious and a tad ornery, but so far no one has threatened to burn me out of my modular bi-level. It was more about the not knowing. It takes a long time for the fire chief and the police to determine the cause of a fire. I never realized just how long until I was waiting with bated breath for the reports. Meanwhile, how could I possibly in good conscience leave the immediate vicinity? I was sure my barn would ignite the minute we crossed the county line. Even the sound of fire sirens in the distance while I was shopping in town was sufficient to send my heart rate spiking. It was a hard-won battle not to drop my groceries and head for home. I confess to texting a neighbor to beg her to pop over to my place and just have a look around, but you didn't hear that from me.

So we stayed home.

Fire wasn't my only concern. There were the badly (in my humble opinion, though the supplier wasn't totally on board with that assessment) rusted propane tanks next to the house to keep me on my last nerve as well. I'm not sure I slept once Cliff pointed them out to me. I'm sure he's sorry he mentioned it at all. If there's anything scarier than the barn (generally empty, with the exception of the mini, which is stalled at night to keep him from becoming bear food, another special concern of mine) bursting into flames, it's the house exploding. Barring turning the place into a bomb, filling the gully below the tanks where the pasture lies with liquid propane would be an equally unhappy turn of events. The horses could die from the exposure, or a wanton human might toss a lit cigarette and light up the whole place like Chinatown on Chinese New Year. I don't allow smoking, either, but I can't be everywhere all the time. I've tried. Just can't do it.

But that's not all! In my herd of lovelies, I harbor mostly geriatric horses. My beloved paint mare, Pokey, is twenty-six now. My even-more-beloved quarter horse gelding, Leo, is twenty-seven. Even Dakota has moved into his twenties since he got here. Zip is sixteen. Duke is fifteen. Even Dolly will be over twenty before the year is out. All of them are a constant source of worry.

None so much, though, as the only boarder horse, Desert Serenade (a.k.a. Pinky, Pinkster, Fuzz Butt, and Hey! I'm Over Here!). Pinky is a completely roaned-out strawberry roan Appaloosa. He has only one eye, and that one has a minor cataract. He's either partially deaf or has an exaggerated startle response to people sneaking up on him. He's got a damaged check ligament behind that makes him walk like a peg-leg pirate. He's got a few teeth that the dentist has proclaimed "wavy" and that are the wonder of the modern scientific world, as Pinky's eating hasn't been impaired despite the dentist's assurance that he can't possibly be processing anything. He's fat, he's sassy, and he's thirty-two.

Pinky is of serious concern because he has "moments." He has knocked himself unconscious, fallen in the barn aisle and gotten wedged between the storage cabinet and the wall, and been known to step backward over rock ledges in his endless search for butt-scratching accommodations.

Of course, if I'm ever going to come home to find a horse in final repose, it's probably not going to be Pinky. He rebounds like a basketball. But I have the sneaking suspicion that one day I'll be away on vacation and get the call that he'd been found lying down in the pasture and someone had him euthanized to put him out of his misery. I've tried to impress on everyone who might be moved to make a life-or-death call on the old boy that they need to (1) make sure he's out of his stall just in case it's for real, and (2) give him an hour. He won't be any more or less dead at that point, but odds are he'll be up and around and none the worse for whatever happened to him. He's funny that way.

In fact, I'm barely recovered from the most recent decision to check the presumed-deceased Pinky for vital signs. Like many old men, he's a very sound sleeper. My poking at him to make sure he was, indeed, gone woke him up, and both of us ricocheted hither and thither about the confines of the ten-by-ten-foot stall until he had his wits about him and I could slide out the door without further injury.

This phone conversation on the first day of our first vacation in a couple of years is typical of life with Pinky:

Barn Hand: [sniffling] I hate to call, but I think Pinky has gone blind.

Me: What makes you think so?

Barn Hand: [sniffling more loudly] He had a hard time getting out of his stall. It's like he couldn't find the door! And he couldn't find the gate to the pasture.

Me: Where is he now? He's not in his stall, right? You know the rule about getting him out of his stall so we don't have to drag him out if he's dead.

Barn Hand: Yes, ma'am! He's outside … [pause to look for the horse] … in the small pen in the barnyard.

Me: And how did he get into the pen? Did you put him there?

Barn Hand: Well, no, I didn't. He walked in on his own. He … uh … [long pause] … he put one over on me again, didn't he?

Me: Bye!

I typed this while a very nice young man replaced my rusted propane tanks, so I can tick that off the list.

On Tuesday, a new (I've used up the others) electrician will come and replace every light fixture in the barn as a preemptive strike against the aging fluorescent fixtures' ballasts burning up and taking the barn with them. He's assured me that my barn is as firesafe as a barn can be, but I know better. Never say those words out loud.

But there's nothing I can do about my old horses. The best I can do is make sure they're also as safe as they can be and make doubly sure that everyone looking after them while I'm away has read the Pinky memo.

Sometime after next Tuesday, I will plan a vacation. I've sworn that, this being my five-year "Yippee! I'm free!" postchemo anniversary after a surprise visit from the big C right after I retired. I will plan something that requires us to go more than three hours' driving time from New Jersey. It might involve an airplane; I'm not sure yet. I've got an image of Bermuda hovering in a semisomnolent brain cell, but I don't know if I'm ready for that. That's not just far; it's across water. In a panicked moment, I wouldn't even be able to rent a car and drive home.

If I'd known that barn ownership led to agoraphobia, would I have bought my own farm? Yes, I probably would have. My mother warned me that sex leads to pregnancy and children, and I did that anyway. And when I think back to the years when my horses were not safe on my hermetically sealed thirty acres but languishing at boarding farms where even feral cats feared to tread, I wonder why paranoia is so much riper now than it was then. I'm opting for aging as a good excuse. It works for so many things; maybe it will do duty in this case too.

I could probably write more about my fears, but you'll have to excuse me now while I double- and triple-check the valves on the new propane tanks. I only checked the feed-room door twice before I left the barn this morning, so I guess a run-by is in order there too. A paranoiac's work is never done!

Good rides are in the heart of the rider.

CHAPTER 6

GOOD RIDES!

I was wandering around Facebook this morning, and I noted that a number of fellow horse people had posted that they'd had a "good ride" on their horses yesterday. I know what that means when my daughter says it. Jess is a talented, fearless rider, tall and limber and competitive as all get-out. Her good ride means her horse was perfect, they spent an hour jumping over tall (by my standards) things and doing fancy dressage moves, and no one was angry when it was over. It occurred to me that I really don't know what other people mean by "good."

In my lexicon, "good" has spread itself over the years to mean a number of different things, depending on the horses, the day, my condition, and to whom I am speaking. If I tell the dressage instructor that I had a good ride on Jess's mare Dolly, it means I managed to sit properly without listing to the right. It means I got more than one stride with her back round and some lightness of being that made my little heart flutter. It means I rode for more than thirty minutes without wanting to cry because I'm not used to that level of concentration for that long. And it means I didn't fall off.

If I tell my daughter, Jess, that I had a good ride on Zip, she knows it means that he actually moved forward, that I didn't yell and scream obscenities to get him to do that, and that we both finished the episode without either of us wanting to send the other to auction.

If I tell my friend and fellow horse person Diana that I had a good ride on Leo, she has no idea what I mean. She has never met Leo except in passing and has no idea what my goals are. If I say the same thing to Jess, she knows I've had another lovefest with the old quarter horse and that we've popped over a few crossrails that could have been five-foot verticals for the level of pleasure I get out of doing that.

If I tell Cliff I had a good ride on Dakota, he's not entirely clear on the details of "good," but he knows I spent some time just happily jogging around the ring pretending either of us knows something about western riding, and he guesses he should have been available for photo ops. He supposes I took those same Leo-safe crossrails in my old barrel saddle and probably ran a few barrels with much fanfare and many loud hoots on my part. Dakota rarely hoots.

That's what my "good rides" look like from the outside. From the inside, their differences are as important as their similarities. My Leo ride is always my best ride, despite the fact that he's twenty-six now and our options are limited. He is my rock. His chestnut coat shines in the sun even when he's filthy, something I've never been able to figure out. When he stands willingly in front of the tack-room door, no halter or tie holding him there, while I dress him for action, there's a peacefulness and joy that's hard to match. When I ride his silky-smooth trot and feel him move into the canter and pull me toward a jump, I'm mindful of never pushing him to do more than he wants to do and grateful that he still wants to do things. Arthritis has taken a toll on both of us, and I want us both to share this amazing bond for as many more years as we can muster. When my stopwatch says we've done twenty or thirty minutes of ring work, I am as happy to ride through the gates and out into the fields and woods as I used to be at hunter paces back in the day. Our hour is plenty, hugs are welcome, and Leo's kisses tell me we're right in tune.

My good rides on Zip are as different from the Leo rides as night is from day. We've had a rough go, Zip and I. His orthopedic issues surrounding a locked rib segued into emotional problems surrounding a fear of pain that took several years and the help of some very smart people to overcome. Just to feel that freight-train engine start up under me without a hitch is enough to make me grin like a toddler with a new toy. Every time we stride on past one of his sticking points, when he moves forward instead of standing still and looking dejected, it's an accomplishment and a thrill, and I can feel him relax into a great friendship recently rekindled. There is still room for improvement, so "good ride" will continue to expand in meaning as time goes by. We may never get back the delirious joyfulness of racing full tilt around a ridiculous jump course I created out of barrels and boards and tarps, but that's the picture I'm shooting for every time I step into the stirrup.

A good ride on Dakota reminds me of a leisurely visit with my best male friend, Mike. We have a shared history, but only to a point. We're old. We're retired. We're at peace. We like learning new things, but we're not insane about it. And if Dakota wants to end the ring time with a wander around the haying equipment to satiate his endless curiosity, that works for me just as much as Mike's desire to end our monthly lunch with a wander through the antique shop across from the restaurant. It's just a quiet, friendly time.

Years ago I had a Three Bars quarter-horse mare and a teenage daughter, and a good ride meant ten miles through woods and down roads and maybe over a fallen log or a pile of tires along the way. It meant a flat-out race on the measured mile along the reclaimed railbed. It was a different kind of ride, and I was a different kind of rider.

I knew I was becoming a "senior rider" the day Jess, after her new horse's dirty stop at a jump landed her in radiology for a wrist X-ray, told me that maybe jumping wasn't all it was cracked up to be. It was an offhand remark in a long phone call about the latest happenings in her corner of the Midwest that told the tale. She said, "You know, I'll be fine with just dressage if he's going to keep up the dirty stops. I don't want to be laid up with the kids to take care of." The surprise part was that she'd purposely spent years seeking out a jumper capable of handily clearing the five-foot jumps she loved so much, and she'd finally found him. Just a couple of years earlier when, unbeknownst to her, she was pregnant with her second child, I had a quiet anxiety attack as I watched her mare go butt-over-saddle on a cross-country course and saw Jess jump back aboard and finish the ride. She was thirty-three when she said that and the mother of two toddlers, proud owner of a long-term care insurance policy and with a new appreciation for the proper alignment of body parts. I was sixty-four and had already noticed that there's a lot to be said for spending as little time as possible on the injured reserve list. I'm not sad about moving into a new category. I can still ride, which is more than I would have predicted back when I was merrily concussing and fracturing and spraining without a care in the world. And I hope to have many, many more good rides, no matter how they look from the outside.

CHAPTER 7

EXCUSES 101

There are times when somehow riding my horses doesn't seem like the best plan in the world. The older I get, the more frequently those times come upon me. And there is always someone nearby who will gleefully point out how much it's costing me to keep the horses and how little progress I'm making in their training and mine. It's not that I owe anyone an explanation—that, after all, is why I got my own farm, so I can make my own rules—but I feel better armed with some ironclad rationale anyway. For those readers who also have moments like those, I offer these elementary excuses. Feel free to apply as needed.

> *My horses are lame.* Yes, all of them. All three riding horses are lame, and the mini's leg looks funny. See how he's holding it?

> *They just had their shots.* What? Are they in pain? Having a reaction? How is that any business of yours? I'm not taking chances, and that's that.

> *They had their feet done yesterday.* I, personally, hate doing anything physical after a pedi, so why would I expect less of my lovely equines? They'll feel better about it if I wait a week.

The sun is out. Until I work up the enthusiasm to coat them all in sunscreen, I will opt to avoid riding in bright sunlight just in case they might get a burn. Burning leads to early aging, wrinkles, and spots. What kind of owner subjects a beloved horse to that sort of abuse, huh?

It's cloudy. Clouds might mean rain, and rain means wet tack, wet horses, and (worst of all) water spots on my very expensive Wal-Mart stretch leggings. I mean, *really!* In whose world is that acceptable?

It's raining. Outstanding! See previous excuse.

It's too hot, cold, boring, windy, snowy, dry, dusty ... pick one and run with it.

My mare foaled. Okay, so it was seventeen years ago, but some of us take longer to get over the trauma than others. I'm still recovering from my episiotomy after thirty-five years.

Look at the time! It's nearly breakfast/lunch/dinner/snack time/dark. Alternatives: "I need to get to work/the market/the spa/the TV room for *Doctor Oz*." Alternatives 2: "My aunt/neighbor/boss/lover/lawyer will be here any minute."

I'm too dirty. Putting on dry-clean-only riding breeches over this layer of sweat and manure would be just plain criminal! I'll need a shower first.

I'm too clean. I just showered and would just hate to get covered in horsehair and dust!

I'm too fat. That week in Bermuda just did me in! As soon as I drop the twenty pounds I put on at the buffet, I'll be right back in the saddle. Really.

I'm too tired. Up all night. Bad stomach. Two hours scouring Marshalls for a new outfit. Who can ride in this condition?

I'm feeling cranky. We all know we should approach our horses in the best possible frame of mind, right? Well, this isn't that frame. It'll be better tomorrow.

The horses are cranky. Yep, they saw the neighbor's dog running along the fence and just got all pissy-assed and out of sorts. They'll be better tomorrow.

My hair looks too good. Would you subject your only good-hair day in a month to helmet head? I didn't *think* so!

It's Thursday. Zip doesn't do Thursdays.

I can't find my no-bounce bra. I just can't deal with a whole hour of a boob-bouncing free-for-all. I'll go see if I can find a new one online.

My stirrups don't feel right. I swear these aren't the ones I've been using. Have you seen any loose stirrups lying around? I think someone stole mine!

Buck *is on HBO!* (No further explanation needed.)

I'm not in the mood. (This one is awfully close to honesty, so save it for special occasions.)

It's important to use excuses sparingly. At the very least, make sure you keep a chart of which horse friends have already heard which of your whines. It doesn't take long to become brown-listed as someone to invite on a ride only under duress … though come to think of it, that's a fine excuse in itself! I'll keep it.

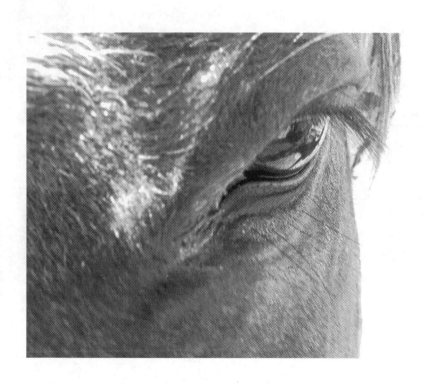

CHAPTER 8

CHANGE, DAMN YOU!

Some time ago I came across an audiobook version of a little self-help number entitled *Switch: How to Change Things When Change Is Hard.* In no way did I expect that Chip and Dan Heath had horse people in mind when they wrote that book. They didn't, of course, but as I listened to their psychosocial theorizing, I found myself nodding and even yelling, "*Yes!* Elephants, riders, and paths ... oh my!"

My mind couldn't help but wander to my big tricolor paint gelding, Zips Furry Butt. Any horse person worthy of the name has at least once in a lifetime come into a training situation that was exciting and confusing, fabulous and frustrating, and that all in one grand sweep pretty much erased his or her self-esteem. Zip was (and still is) my eraser.

Over the years things happened between the Zipster and me. Good things, like happy trail rides and great show results, were followed by bad things, like his "rodeo year," when every ride ended in a bucking spree, followed by more good things and so on. We'd reached a détente, which is sometimes the best one can hope for. I'd gotten some help from other books and other professionals to whom I am eternally grateful, as they allowed me to stop embarrassing myself in front of my horse. Whether or not he was actually laughing at me is moot. It felt that way to me, and that's what mattered.

Then *Switch* happened.

So there I was with a horse I adored who had the best attitude (about some things) and was the most fun (sometimes) and who could delight me to laughter or bring me to tears, sometimes simultaneously, and I heard a voice coming from my car speaker say, "Don't be an archaeologist" or something to that effect. Well, *duh!* I'm an equestrian, a follower of the Path of the Black Stallion (don't google that; I made it up), member of the Sisterhood of the Traveling First-Aid Kit. Archaeology was nowhere in my resume.

I clicked the button to replay the chapter since I hadn't really been listening (like my horses, what's on my mind most often is pretty much nothing), and I prepared to talk back to the speakers as is my private habit. Then I noticed that the author wasn't talking about archaeology in the sense of digging through the manure pile to find my ancient lost cell phone. This was psychological archaeology he was warning against, as in "Don't waste your time on what happened in the past to cause the present problem; just solve the damned thing as quickly as possible."

Now, this is a concept I could get behind with both muck boots. I'd already spent years apologizing to Zip, theorizing about the genesis of his various quirks and my part in their formation. And I'd begun the new riding season with Buck Brannaman's words nagging at the back of my brain. Just before his faithful helper was mauled by an out-of-control stallion in the movie *Buck*, he'd told the man to stop worrying about how the stud might act and "ride him like he's your grandmother's trail horse." Granted, it didn't work out real well on that particular occasion, but for the most part it's good advice.

Horses are sensitive critters, and they sense your tension and fear. Mount up expecting a blowup, and you're likely to get one. I'd already worked the big boy from the ground to get his muscles back in shape after a long winter of relaxation, and on the third day, armed with several bags of my favorite calming-and-focusing supplement (for Zip … mine doesn't come in bags) and a new saddle pad (my nod to magical thinking that just one more pad or saddle or whatever will make the difference), I'd hopped aboard as if he were my grandmother's trail horse.

Sadly, my grandmother didn't have a horse, but I approached Zipper as if nothing bad had ever happened between us, and as hoped, he pre-tended right back at me. What ho! We had liftoff, and the crowd in my head (it does get crowded in there) roared with approval.

Still, in a soft spot to the left of my right ear was all the bad stuff I'd squirreled away. All the balkiness, all the orthopedic issues, even the bucking that happened more than a decade ago were all still there until I pulled the plug and stopped being an archaeologist. What an amaz-ing thing! In one click of a "switch," I was right there in the moment engaged in actual problem solving instead of harrying the past, hoping for something to flash for me and change the circumstances.

What the Heaths were talking about was a psychotherapy theory that, unlike the older Freudian model that took years of couch work and blaming one's mother to unearth the boo-boos on one's inner child and heal them, focuses on the here and now and what can be done to effectively change the behavior that's problematic. All the rest—all the self-denigration, recriminations, woulda-coulda-shoulda stuff—is hurled into a drawer with the label "TBU," "True, But Useless." It's true that I was a little slow in rooting out Zip's orthopedic problems, but that fact doesn't move the change process forward one smidge. Knowing he has those issues, now there's a nut worthy of hoarding. Leave out the "if only" and go with the "here it is."

That's not the only utter coolness the Heaths have to share. There's the elephant part. I truly love that image. Picture an elephant, a rider, and a path. In order to effect change, one must motivate the elephant (right, emotional brain), direct the rider (left, analytical brain), and make the path clear. "See. Feel. Change." Whoa!

Zip: Is that elephant thing a thinly veiled reference to the size of my butt? If so, I am deeply offended.

Me: Nope, this is not about you.

Zip: Okay then. Can I have a cookie?

Your mother-in-law's right brain is the elephant in the room. You want your mother-in-law to stop criticizing the way you allow the decorative peanut-butter smear to remain on the kitchen wall. That's an emotional subject. She can't stand the mess and feels that deeply. The highly sensitive elephant needs motivation, so you find something that will make it want to change direction. Perhaps it's a fun-loving elephant that might enjoy an outing with you and the peanut-butter artiste. There's the motivation. It's also what the Heaths refer to as a "destination postcard"—a picture of the coolness that awaits the change at the end of the path.

Next you have to direct the rider, who, left to her own devices, will dither and analyze and get nowhere in a hurry. You have a destination and her emotional elephant at hand. You need to get the analytical right-brained rider on board with your plan. She needs clear, uncomplicated directions. Not "I wish you'd stop doing that." That's not clear direction. That's too fuzzy and offers too many possible alternative behaviors, such as picking on your inability to keep the green mold in the fridge from flinging open the door and exposing itself to the neighbors. That's not helpful to your plan. Too many choices lead to "decision paralysis" and no choice at all.

No, to direct the rider, you have to have a clear path in mind and give her clear and concise direction. Not "be a nicer person," but "tell me how much you love the way I'm raising your grandkids." No fuzziness, just a simple instruction.

Finally, you need to remove obstacles from the path so there is no question where this team is headed. Have your social interactions at her peanut-butter-free house for a while, for instance, and the rest will be easy. Her analytical rider will push her emotional elephant down the clear path to the destination shown on the postcard.

With Zip, it's a lot clearer than the peanut-butter scenario. The elephant in our room is his anxiety, which leads to balkiness. I want him to not balk. In positive terms—something that is "actionable"—I want him to walk forward without my having to beg. At this early stage of correction, I'm not even going to get into his level of enjoyment, which I hope will eventually return to prior levels. I just want one thing to change.

To motivate this particular elephant, there are two options. He's big on food treats, so the clicker and the belt bag filled with Frosted Mini-Wheats is an easy cue. He's already on board with that; it's just a matter of connecting it to the desired change. I've already done that, and like the TV chef who just passes quickly over how that ten-layer cake with fondant icing shaped like a swan evolved, I'll skip the details. Let's just say, "Then something happened."

His other motivating force, given the pain and discomfort issues he still vividly remembers (kissing spines, locked rib, chiropractic adjustment), is R&R. He dearly loves being told he's wonderful and then being offered free naked grazing time on the front lawn. So as we segue away from the stimulus-response training so that I don't have to remember to strap on the feed bag, we pick up the postperformance standing ovation and grass-bouquet toss.

That's one elephant, one destination, two motivations. Check.

Now the driver—Zip's little pea-sized analytical brain—needs direction, clear and uncomplicated. He's a born anticipator, which means he overthinks everything. This is where task analysis is a big player. Breaking it down, I want him to:

Stand still while I tack him up

Stand still at the mounting block while I mount

Walk away without any hint of balkiness

You might notice that there's a lot of standing still in my plan, so that's my focus for most of the directions. Then there's a transition from standing still (which requires a reward first) to walking.

Finally, there's the clearing of the path. If there's something physically standing in his way, Zip isn't going to do what I'm asking. That's pretty simple when you're dealing with horses. If I put the mounting block too close to his legs, he won't walk. If I put it too far away, he won't stand still. Finding the right spot is important, and we've pretty much got that licked. As for the moving forward piece, we can't wind up mounted and facing the fence. That's a great excuse for no forward movement, or total hysteria because the choices are too complicated. So I make sure there's literally nothing standing in his way.

That's all there is to it. If you want someone to change, it's your job to make it as easy as possible. Preload the questionnaire with all the pertinent information so the respondent only has to tick yes or no.

On your own side of the equation, it's interesting to note that research has shown unequivocally that bad stuff has staying power while good stuff fades fairly quickly. So you're going to have to do some work to get the bad memories out of your head before you approach that elephant. According to the Heaths, this is called "positive-negative asymmetry." This is why it's easier to hate someone more the longer it's been since you've seen them. The good stuff fades away, and the bad comes to the forefront. So it is with our horses. We easily recall every detail of our last unplanned horizontal girth inspection, but the fine points of the wonderful time we were having just before Fuzzbutt went vertical are hazy. When was the last time you heard people give a lengthy description of every amazingly beautiful and balanced step their horse took leading up to the dirty stop at the fence? Usually that level of detail is reserved for the slo-mo tumble that fractured someone's arm or cost someone a ribbon. Try it.

Successful change is easier to achieve if you stop focusing on the bad behavior and focus on the few times you got the response you hoped for. The Heaths call this looking for the "bright spots." If your horse acted up two out of every seven times you tried to put him to a particular task, instead of calculating what was happening when he acted up, concentrate on the five good times and figure out what was going on *then*—what were you and he doing right—because that's the behavior you want to replicate. Trying to figure out what *not* to do is too big an arena. There are too many choices. Picture putting a child in a room with one piece of candy on a table and, without directions to clear the path, taking away the candy every time the child does anything other than recite the alphabet backward. Finding that one positive solution by trial and error is a frustrating and overwhelming task. Eventually the child will quit trying or will get angry and beat you with the table.

You need to figure out the few things that you *should* do instead. It cuts down on that confusion and asymmetry and gives you a goal as meaningful as the one you're giving your horse (or your spouse or your teenager or the child with the candy dilemma). I've gotten the best response from Zip when I approached him without a serious agenda and without a boatload of *shoulds* crowding my brain. When the only thing I hoped for was that he would let me mount without a lengthy gavotte around the mounting block to wear my nerves thin, then I got a lot more because I wasn't as stressed and I could make my goal simple and clear.

As soon as the cold snap is over and I'm back outdoors, I intend to bleed my mind of every bubble of negativity and focus on the things I can do right with Zip. Stand back and watch us change!

CHAPTER 9

Ω

ADVANCED EXCUSES (EXCUSES 201)

For advanced riders who ride often, ride in shows, and require bigger and better excuses due to their place in the riding hierarchy, disallowing fear of riding as a viable excuse, the following alternatives will suffice. Again, use these sparingly to avoid removing yourself and your horse from party guest lists.

It's too close to show day. I sure as heck don't want Fuzzbutt overworked and crabby for our classes! That would be a surefire ribbon-buster.

It's more than a week before show day. If I work Last Call today, by next week he'll have forgotten everything. I just hate to waste time on pointless training!

My trainer said not to overdo the lateral work. Since I can't think of anything else to do, I'll just give us both a day off. Darn!

My trainer isn't available. I'm working at the highest level of extended amble, transitioning into spook with squeal. I certainly wouldn't want to practice the wrong aids and wind up screwing up my horse. Would you?

He's got a wind puff. It could turn into a full-out body puff if I'm not careful, so I'm giving him the month off. Make that two, in fact. No sense taking chances!

I think there's a saddle-fitting problem. I ordered a new saddle and pad and bridle and boots and grooming supplies from five different catalogs in three foreign countries. As soon as it all gets here, and assuming it all fits and matches, I'll hop up and give him a whirl.

I just read an article. It doesn't matter what it was about. I'm sure somewhere in there it said I need a few weeks of yoga meditation before I try riding Wing Nut again.

I haven't found the right music. Freestyle dressage routines set to music just absolutely hinge on finding exactly the right tunes and getting the right choreographer. I'm working on it.

He's ready for the piaffe. I'm not.

He's breathing funny. In … out … in … out … Does that seem right to you?

He gave me the stink eye again. No way am I getting on him.

I can't find my cell phone. What if I fall off? What if he has a seizure? What if I overhear some really ripe gossip? How will I be able to call anyone without my phone? I'll ride again when I've found it.

I think he's gone deaf! Did you see how he ignored me when I called to him in the pasture? I'd better not ride him until the vet can look at him.

Was that a squirrel or a wolf? If I heard it, he must have, and you know how he gets about predators lurking in the trees.

He's having a bad day. Just look at those sad eyes! You can just see how depressed he is. I wouldn't dream of getting on him when he's feeling down in the dumps. Horses have feelings too, you know.

She bucked me off yesterday. 'Nuff said.

My chi is out of balance. Flow is everything!

We're working on ground manners. Yes, it's been a year, but look how well he stands still now! Next we're going to do standing still without biting me.

My trainer quit. Sorry. There will be no riding until she stops ignoring my texts and tells me what to do.

He's not in the mood. Sometimes I can just tell, and this is one of those times. No, I don't have to actually go to the barn to know this. I can feel it. I'm sensitive like that.

I'm not in the mood. (This moves from beginner to advanced excuse when it's said with conviction and a snarl.)

CHAPTER 10

⟨horseshoe symbol⟩

SPECIAL AILMENTS OF SENIOR HORSES

This chapter should not by any stretch of anyone's imagination supplant your vet manual or the practitioner you've got on speed dial. This is merely a summary of some of the conditions and consternations that only senior horses bring to the table. Consider it an addendum to the chapter in my 2007 book *Horses in the Yard*.

Antifibularium: In every gang of elderly equines, there will always be one whose continued existence is in question moment by moment. It doesn't matter how expensive and high-quality your stethoscope might be, hearing this fellow's heartbeat is impossible. The mellow thubbing is not only inaudible, but is overwhelmed by unidentifiable noises that resemble, in ensemble, a garage band working on a new song. There is no treatment.
Prognosis: Extreme longevity.

Hairsuitism: This is unrelated to any other syndrome. Old horses just don't want to let go of their hair until they are certain that winter is entirely over or that you are wearing the new power suit for which you slapped down a month's pay. When they're sure, they will let all of their hair go at once in Velcro clumps. The treatment of choice is a gaggle of neighborhood kids armed with shedding combs.
Prognosis: Corduroy aversion in all handlers.

Pedometry: Horses are generally born with four feet, and in young horses, all four tend to grow hoof wall at a reasonably consistent rate. Not so in older horses. Geriatric equines can control their hoof growth so that only one hoof will grow this month, making conversations with your farrier awkward and a little unproductive. Even the most under-standing shoers will raise an eyebrow when asked to drive forty miles to trim one hoof. There is no treatment.
Prognosis: Eighteen farriers on speed dial, none of whom will pick up the phone.

Antipedometry: On the flip side of the pedometry issue stands the antique horse, who will allow all feet to grow at once, but only twice a year and only when you have finally decided you can afford to go on a vacation without risking returning to a deceased equine. The day before you leave, he will let all of his feet grow a minimum of three inches of new hoof, which will require immediate trimming. No treatment is necessary other than trimming.
Prognosis: No vacations, ever.

Longifornia: Aging males of many species—horses in particular—lose the ability to care about the condition of their private parts and will let them flail in the wind for all to see, particularly when standing for judging in a halter class in the hands of a very, very young new show rider. Your niece will be horrified, which is part of the joy of this part of learning about horses. Don't bother reprimanding your elderly horse buddy. He won't care. There is no treatment.
Prognosis: Intense joy on breezy days.

Penippearance: The gelding suffering from this particular condition will happily let his grimy schlong linger for a breath of fresh air until the moment you pull on your rubber gloves for a good sheath clean-ing. It pays to buy the gloves vets use to palpate mares' uteruses—the elbow-length number—because that's how far you'll be into the job before you can approach ground zero with your goo-soaked cotton

wad. Treatment: Call the vet and arrange a "sheath and teeth" day so the horse will be drugged into allowing this indignity.
Prognosis: Full recovery and big vet bills.

Crust: On the occasions when a gelding is waving his stuff in the open air, savvy owners may sometimes catch a glimpse of something that looks like gray Post-its hanging from it. This crust is the accumulated swag from many a roll in the ring footing or the muck next to the hay feeder. It can also represent the less-than-stellar urination efforts of an old guy too lazy to let it drop before he empties his bladder. Some elder geldings wear it as a point of pride to show their compatriots that they can still get down and dirty and back up again without requiring a hoist and two burly vet techs. Some just have a what-the-hell attitude. Save this for "sheath and teeth" day, when the vet will administer happy juice that will allow the dentist to float what few rock-hard teeth are left while the vet manhandles the crust off Pappy Dan's privates.
Prognosis: Clean, happy guy with a fondness for the vet.

Dentigranosis: Around the age of consent, a horse's teeth become questionable in intent and condition. When the horse dentist tells you he needs to have the vet give Sparky a shot so he'll stop clamping his jaws and let the work be done, just suck it up and go for it. Did you know that horses' teeth just grow for so long and then quit? The instant they quit growing, they wear down, while simultaneously turning rock-hard. It can take several very large dentists with power equipment to successfully wrestle down an old horse and file down sharp points on his teeth, and he will hold you personally responsible. Since nothing is more vindictive than an old horse, it's better to pay the vet and have the old geezer relaxed and happy so that whatever remains of his teeth can be made reasonably useful on his feed, not on your upper arm when your back is turned. Treatment: Regular floating, even if it takes two dentists with a jackhammer to get the job done. Lots of soaked feed.
Prognosis: Eventually he'll just, as we all must, die.

Feel free to rip out this chapter and tuck it in the back of whatever vet manual you have at hand. It is not meant to replace sane veterinary advice, just to add a few ailments that only horse owners will ever know about. Some day veterinary medicine will catch up.

CHAPTER 11

Ω

HOSPITAL OR HOSPICE?

A few years ago, I wrote an article with this title for a medical advice website. It was about humans, of course, and whether it's better to stick Grandpa in the hospital when he reaches the point where he's beyond any management you can sanely deliver or to let him stay home with the services of the local hospice fully engaged in his care. With humans, it's a bit of an easier decision. The law doesn't provide for irritated spouses to call the doctor to come and give a lethal injection. For a human to qualify for hospice care, he or she must be formally declared incurable and terminal by a physician with an actual license. Cranky offspring are not allowed to make that determination.

It occurred to me that the same question is just as valid (maybe more so, since we are allowed to make life-or-death decisions for our animals that the law prevents us from making for our relatives) for horse owners. Is it better to ship Sir Doggerel off to a major vet clinic when he appears to be approaching the pearly pasture gates, or is he better off at home with someone knowledgeable taking care of him until he leaves the planet?

There is no easy answer to this, though an awful lot of people will offer one. I've noticed this phenomenon as regards my long-retired black-and-white paint mare, Pokey, who has a number of ailments on her CV that have big, nasty names and very poor prognoses. Not the least of these is squamous cell carcinoma, or as we like to call it, given its location on her vulva, "rotting nethers."

Depending on the proclivities and horse sense of the respondent, my description of the state of Pokey's health and the treatment being applied receives widely varied comments. Most nonhorse people are good for a sigh and a "poor thing." They opt not to go further in their assessment because they have no idea what I'm talking about. The horse lovers who have never owned a horse or had to make life-or-death decisions regarding any beloved animal offer support at levels ranging from "Isn't that nice of you" to "That's a lot of work, but there's a place in heaven for you" to "You're kidding! You had laser surgery and chemo on a *horse*?"

The horse fanatics who might have owned a horse at some time in the past urge further exploration of the remarkably expensive avenues available to me. These are the folks who generally litter their commentary with malapropisms for which they can be forgiven because they haven't ever seen the words written, only heard them spat out by elder horsemen in days long gone. They tend to fall into the alive-at-all-costs category and need to be taken with a grain of salt.

The ones who own horses now know all the latest research by heart and are determined to share with me their expertise, which I fully appreciate. Really. That's not a joke. I can't possibly read everything there is out there, so anyone—like the horse dentist who had amazing results in reducing a tumor using Crest toothpaste—can chime in, and I'll give solid consideration to the suggestions.

But the sanest of all are the true horsemen, currently horsed or not, who invariably ask the right question, the one that gets me to stop throwing solutions at the problem and think about what I'm doing. My Facebook friend Mike put it best:

"Are you doing this for her or for you?"

Every now and then when I'm writing the day's instructions for the barn hands on the board and there's something regarding meds for Pokey or a particular issue I need to have reported to me immediately, those words come back to me. I've said them to other horsemen, but it sounds different coming from the outside. For whom am I doing this, and at what point should I stop?

I have answered that to my own satisfaction several times. If a bute tab is enough to stop her tail-wringing—the outward sign that her tumor is acting up and she's feeling cranky about it—then it's for her sake. She eats. She sleeps. She chases Pinky the One-Eyed Wonder App away from the hay feeder. She's fat and sassy. She's fine, and I'm giving her more days in the sun as painlessly as possible. But the other day when she came in late for breakfast, which she has never done in the seventeen years of our relationship, I had to stop for a minute and think. It turned out that she'd simply been distracted and that I needed to give her a bute to get her through her monthly cycle, which always makes her problem a little worse, but I truly began in those moments to plan for the future. Another winter? Another year? Or will fall shots for everyone bring that special blue liquid in her syringe?

Today she's fine. The pain relief did its job and made her a happy girl again. Tomorrow she might not be. At some point, the tumor will cross the threshold, and the choice will be obvious. I have promised myself and my lovely mare that I won't wait till she's stopped eating and is dwindling to a mere rack of hide-covered bone. When she stops being queen of the hay feeder, her time here will be done, and we'll take the next step together. I prefer to see my animals off personally, though that hasn't always been possible. So I'll be there with her, cookies in hand. Her immense and obvious spirit demands that. She'll be brushed to a shine, her mane combed, and her warm eyes looking into mine. And she'll go before the pain makes her wish she could. That's my gift to my animals, and it's their gift to me that they stay with me as long as they can.

(*Note*: As I edit this chapter some months after it was written, Pokey has gone on to her end. There came a point when there was no longer a question as to whether or not she was in pain. She was, and it was time for her to go in peace. She'll be missed, but I'm happy that she missed the worst of the pain that would have come for her.)

CHAPTER 12

REINVENTING YOUR INNER HORSEMAN

This is a very important thought:

> *"The stories we tell ourselves make our problems worse. Without the story line, the problem has no energy to survive."* (Laura King, life coach)

This has been a year of transition, and it's not over yet. For the country, for the world, there have been changes aplenty. It's 2013, and over the past twelve months, battles have raged in the Middle East and elsewhere. Populations have been ravaged, and others have found new ground to move forward onto. Women's rights are a hot-button topic, and rightly so. Animal rights are not as burning a subject, but it's on the stove and being addressed with changes in laws and the rooting out of errant and fraudulent charities. What a year!

For my part, I really could have used a little less change.

A few months ago I attended a "Ladies' Retreat" (I seriously hate the word *ladies* as applied to gatherings of women mostly in gym clothes and universally cranky) at the local community college. This fund-raising and consciousness-raising event is an annual effort to raise money to send girls to college. It has the bonus effect of reminding me, at least, why gatherings of "ladies" are to be approached with calculated caution. There is learning to be done above the cacophony of complaints about the number of snacks and quality of entertainment served up.

As part of the program, I attended a lecture by motivational speaker Laura King titled "Reinventing Yourself When Life Changes." It sounded like just the thing to help me get past my traitorous daughter's planned move to a state farther than a day's driving distance away and my own body's decision to age all at once instead of following the piecemeal plan I'd devised for it.

The first thing Ms. King said made my ears prick up and my nose twitch. She said, "Every moment dies so the next can be born. Impermanence and uncertainty are necessary for us to change, learn, and grow."

Whoa! Thank you, Ms. King, for putting my entire package of daily terror into such a neat analytical statement.

It took a few thoughtful moments for the reality of that to sink in. Fighting change is my stock-in-trade. It's what I do best, despite my effort to make it look like I ebb and flow without a second thought. I change quickly and easily, but not without a lot of backward glances. I'm quick on the decision button and slow to give up explaining to myself why what I'm doing is right and reasonable. I'm a tough sell on my own stories sometimes.

As a horseman, much of the change in my life revolves around my horses and my riding. That has been the focus of much of my aging angst. When I spend more time making excuses not to ride than I do in the saddle, I have to rethink my motives, and that's where I was when I happened to hear the stories comment that started this chapter.

We all tell ourselves and other people stories. We tell stories about who we are, who they are, why we're better than they are, and why someone else needs to die a nasty and untimely death to make our lives more livable. And boy, do we have stories about our horses! Our love-hate relationship with the horse world is clear in the way we talk about the challenges in our training and riding situations.

That got me thinking. My current story is that I'm a very good (not excellent) rider and trainer. I'm sadly laboring under the persistent aging of my body (my inner child hasn't aged a day, thanks) and those of my horses. I don't need to compete anymore because I've been there and done that and lost interest when it turned into work. I don't really need to get my horses into shape for riding this spring because it's unlikely I'll do much anyway given all the excuses I've spent so much time crafting. I'll get myself into shape when I get around to it, and I'm not suffering from some ailment that gives me yet another excuse not to do the hard parts.

I'm a mother, a horseman, a hard worker, a writer. I'm a caretaker, a family member, a teacher, a farmer. And I'm impermanent on this planet, as are we all. I'm sure I serve a purpose, but I'm not clear what that might be at this juncture. I'm too old to care about a lot of things and too young for that not to piss me off.

> *"Energy is wasted in the fiction we make up. Our pain becomes our universe, but millions of other beings are feeling the same thing."* (King)

Fiction? What the hell?

Yes, fiction. All of the stories I tell are fictional. The truth—the *real me*—is just a mound of cells, rapidly deteriorating, housing a questioning (and often questionable) spirit. The truth is silent and pretty much invisible to the naked eye. It only shows up during moments of meditation, and it takes some effort to quiet my mind enough to hear the truth.

With that in mind, I headed out to the lower pasture, where my advisory council was grazing. I have fictions about them too. Even though they can't hear the stories I tell, they can read them in my body and in the way I relate to them.

Zip: Here she comes, queen of the world. She looks spirited. She's going to want to make me do something I don't want to do. I'm so out of here!

Kota: Hey! She could have cookies! When she walks like that, there are usually cookies, so I'm sticking around until I can get a whiff of her pocket.

Leo: I don't see a halter. She doesn't have a halter, guys! What in hell is she up to with no halter?

Pokey: I'm going to stand right near her. Here … No, here … No …

She's sitting on a rock. That's not right. She's not a rock-sitter. I'll just sniff her hair and see if it's really her.

For the past few years, I've approached my training program with a hit-or-miss, it's-all-their-fault kind of attitude, peppered with occasional self-loathing when I realize I'm the cause of most of the horses' issues. Stories about stories are what these are. On this day, I'm not interested in stories. I'm interested in quiet and in hearing my reality and theirs. So in service to that, I don't say anything. I quiet my mind and just stand with the horses.

A few years back, a famous trainer wrote that if we want to be horsemen, we need to spend time—just time, not activity—hanging in the pasture with our horses. He seemed to be suggesting days of that, not just a few minutes, and he lost me at that point as I'd long since stopped telling the story about the outdoorsman me. But in spirit, he was right. As I stood silently in the pasture, the horses at first cocked an ear toward me but didn't give me any attention. The body language of herd dynamics: ignore the outlier and she'll go away. Within minutes, though, Pokey, who couldn't resist human contact (bet she had some story to cover that particular foible), ambled over to stick her nose in my face. I petted said nose, and with the ice broken and jealousy afoot, Zip and Dakota rushed to get their face time too.

For once, I just enjoyed the moment on a sunny day in the shade of the trees, where the horses have carved out their loafing area without passing judgment on Zip for being pushy ("He thinks he's the leader, but he's such a wuss" is the story I tell about him most often, followed by a lengthy mental diatribe about how much I miss how he and I used to be together and the anger and frustration and yada, yada, yada) and without mentally commenting on how the others looked or didn't look, behaved or didn't behave. For that brief moment, I could hear clearly who they were.

What a delightful moment that was! It was cool beyond words. It didn't last because my mind is story-addicted, so I *had* to decide who needed to be ridden and what we would work on and why (there's always a *why* to justify the story). But for a moment, there it was, and it really was peaceful and quiet.

I've had those moments in the past but without the intention. It is my intention (story time!) to do that more often.

One day all this will be my grandson's (but the bills will be his parents').

Training horsemen isn't just about horses.

CHAPTER 13

PLAY IT AGAIN, SAM ... PLEASE

I was standing in the barn waiting for Zip to finish chewing his lead rope and reading one of the glossy horse mags when a letter to the editor got me thinking. Everything old is new again, and we can't quite get past the past to accept the present. My mind really got cranking when I read the plea to get more kids involved with horses. The writer suggested that horse owners need to share their horses and their addiction with greater enthusiasm, so that more children will fall in love with the big hairy beasts and the sports surrounding them.

That, naturally, brought to mind the utter joy with which, back in 1959, my parents greeted my interest in horses. Dad laughed uncomfortably and left the room. I can still see Mom's horrified expression. I'll never know whether her face reflected a fear for my safety, her terror at the thought of horse-produced dirt, or the fact that she was about to be doomed to many hours of chauffeur duty. Avidly driving-averse, to that point she'd managed to avoid such unpleasantness. Unlike today, the 1950s did not require women to possess drivers' licenses or cars, let alone run taxi services for their offspring. Those truly were more peaceful times.

In any case, Dad's laughter, however inscrutable, put the stamp of approval on my horse life. I stopped sending in non–parentally approved entries to the "Name This Filly" contest, one of the many giveaway come-ons that dotted newspapers' Sunday supplements back in the 1950s and which gave parents of the day a much older appearance than today's tend to have, and started taking lessons. Life was never the same. At least my parents no longer had to worry about where to house the baby racehorse I was trying to win. They only needed to cross over into a world not of their making.

My heart goes out to the moms of horse kids, since I both had one and became one later. Those early Saturday drives forty minutes to the lesson barn for an 8:00 a.m. group lesson could not have been what Mom signed up for when she married an up-and-coming corporate type. That she "watched" my lessons with her back turned, seated in her car, which was parked at the top of the barn driveway as far from the action as physically possible without a helicopter, suggests certain trepidation. In her defense, she didn't start out that far away. The first couple of weeks, she sat facing the ring and watched stone-faced while we kiddos raced hell-bent around our hunt-coated instructor, who shouted commands that none of us seemed able to follow. But a few near misses pretty much did her in.

Still, she was fortunate. Back in those days, there weren't many indoor arenas, so lessons started in May and ended in September, when the New Jersey horses were shipped to sunny Florida to be campers for the winter. And one lesson per week was all that was expected. In fact, it was all that was possible given the unlighted riding areas and the fact that parents didn't fall for the "you need three lessons a week if you intend to be competitive" thing. My brother got one Boy Scout meeting a week and I got one riding lesson, and that was that. Anything we could do on foot or by bicycle without benefit of parental involvement was an automatic go; anything else, not so much.

So when I saw a plea to get more kids involved, my first thought wasn't for the kids or the horses; it was for the poor, beleaguered moms. And let's not forget the dads, who in this age of continued wage inequality between the sexes, are still more likely to shoulder the expense of little Lucy's equine fetishism. Today, that can more than equal a mortgage payment, and there's no house at the end of that cash-paved road. In fact, the house is just as likely to fall prey to the ills that come of overextension, and not in the dressage sense.

By the time I was old enough to have a horse and a horse kid of my own, not only had my eyes been pried open by the bills attached to that lifestyle, but the times had changed as well. There was no more "lessons available." There was "lessons mandatory" as a stipulation of boarding an equine pet at a prestigious horse hotel with all the comforts of home and some theretofore unimagined. In exchange, the equine in question might be treated to daily brushing, fans and heaters as needed, and a brass nameplate on the front door of his stall, and all involved got all the snobbery they could stomach. It wasn't just riding once a week and being thrilled at the opportunity. It was riding every day and playing snot-faced-attitude games with the other horse moms. It was designer clothes all around. When I grew up, Miller's was *the* name in riding clothes. Now there are so many names that are de rigueur in the world of equestrian couture that I can't keep up.

Fortunately my daughter is not so impaired, so when she goes gaga over something I've never heard of from a catalog I've never seen at a price she says is amazing and I think is obscene, I can take notes for future gifting. Not to be entirely outdone, I will confess that along with my Wal-Mart leggings, my person this summer will be graced by a brand-new helmet of the One K line with (ready?) *retractable sun visor*. No more sunglasses sliding down my sweaty nose to perch embarrassingly on my upper lip. I aim to thrill the squirrels, and the UPS guy has got to be able to see the gleam of that gloss finish as he unloads my next pile of horse-related purchases. What that helmet set me back would have fed my mother's 1950s' family for six months.

Much as I would love to leap on the bandwagon and blindside unsuspecting friends by luring their children into this horse life, I just don't have it in me. When I think about how many months peanut butter on celery stalks was an acceptable meal for myself and my child because the board on a couple of horses was sucking my paycheck right out of my hand, I get a little sad. We survived and we enjoyed it all, but we were occasionally on the edge of financial ruin, and that's not the kind of "edge" horse people generally aim for.

I'll let the rest of you act as emissaries from the horse world to the real world. I'll let kids pet my horses and I'll give the occasional pony ride, but I'm not going to suck another mother into the black hole to stand next to my daughter, who is currently raising her own budding horse person. I escaped relatively unscathed, but not unscarred. The next mom might not be so lucky.

My mother put up with my terrible know-it-all attitude when she brought a friend along on our only attempt to watch *the* big state horse show, and I couldn't resist making it known that she was totally clueless and that I would *not* be answering stupid questions, thank you very much. I was nothing if not very sixteen. I put up with my own child's mouthiness just once and just briefly when she announced that I was something short of perfect on the night before a show. I told her she had two choices. She could accept that I had horse friends who actually liked riding with me and who would gladly substitute while she sat home glowering, or she could apologize and be ready at six in the morning with a smile and a happy word. Experience had already taught me that shutting that down immediately was the best thing I could do for both of us. I'd seen a young rider slap her mother right in the show ring for bringing her the wrong gloves before her class. That mother would *not* be me. And it wasn't.

Moms have it rough enough. Moms and dads are underwater financially and emotionally already. They need a break. Convincing little Lucy that she just *has* to have riding lessons, a horse, a bunch of horses, a horse farm, a spot in a pricey private school where horses are curricular ... that's just not fair. Parents today are at a disadvantage, as someone sometime along the path to the twenty-first century gave them a lobotomy. It might have happened right in the delivery room, hard to say. Since they can't say no all on their own, I'm going to say it for them by not saying yes in the first place.

They'll thank me later, I assure you.

And if you want to rant at me for not doing my part to find homes for unwanted horses, I beg you to visit a horse rescue of the sanctuary type. Look at the abandoned and abused horses, not with a sappy, "Awwww!" but with a "Wow! Somebody bought a horse they couldn't afford to keep and didn't know enough to maintain, and here it is looking skinny and sad. I sure don't want to be someone who does that." When you look at it with those eyes, it's a different picture entirely. It doesn't take Photoshop to take myself out of that picture, just common sense. This year I'm putting common sense on my horseman's must-have list.

CHAPTER 14

LOVE IN BLOOM

Leo is smitten. His object of desire is Dolly. They are thwarted by an-other, who simply delights in keeping them apart. This would sound like the plotline for a Broadway musical if it weren't that two of the characters are horses and horses don't sing very well.

In an earlier chapter, I noted that my daughter's thoroughbred mare Baby Doll was coming home to my farm to retire, and so she did. As I write this essay, it's been a week since she returned, and a very interesting week I must say. There is always a bit of anxiety involved in introducing a new horse to an established herd, even when the horse isn't entirely unfamiliar to the rest of the pasture's citizens. Bringing a mare into a mostly-gelding enclave has its own issues revolving around sex, mood, attitude, and … well … sex. Even the neutered have their fantasies, and mares are always left intact so you know there are hormones at play on the female side.

It didn't surprise me that my big paint, Zip, was the first to exhibit a rather intense interest in Dolly. There was a lot of snorting and chuff-ing and posturing for the first three days. He stopped by her stall with a "Hey, baby! *Whazzup?*" going and coming. For the first day he could not be pried away from the fence separating her temporary pen from the main pasture. I had a feeling we were in for a long haul, with Zip in charge of the settling-in process.

But I was mistaken. Zip's mom, Pokey, eventually stepped in and rather violently, with teeth bared and hind feet flying, pointed out to her son that the age difference (he's sixteen; Dolly is twenty-one) was inappropriate, and besides, he has no equipment with which to seal the deal. There was a visible settling down all around, and Dolly joined the herd. She took possession of the one-eyed Appy, who will be eternally grateful as she, even sporadically, prevented Pokey from driving him away from the hay and dictating where he could and couldn't stand in the pasture. He's feeling more rested already. I swear he has put on twenty pounds.

She also adopted the big-butted Appy, Dakota, who is so laid-back it was hard to tell that there had been a sea change in his world. He just kind of meandered over the line that divides Pokey's herd from Dolly's. Dolly is a much kinder queen, so I can't blame him. She rules with a glance, where Pokey always has to take it to the ears-back, teeth-bared level.

But the process didn't get really interesting until the first night I let the newcomer stay out with the herd. I kept her stalled the first three nights due to questionable weather and a more pressing question as to whether or not she would come back in with them in the morning, but the fourth night was clear and warm and the same was predicted for the morning, so at least I wouldn't be chasing down a frolicking horse in the driving rain should she decide she liked her freedom. On that night, she and Leo got some prolonged face time, and that's all they needed.

Leo is twenty-seven. I didn't think he had it in him to be highly emotional about anything, let alone a mare he'd known for eight years prior to her seven-year relocation to Pennsylvania. I've thought about it for days, and I don't ever recall them being an item back then. Dolly belonged to my daughter's dominant gelding, Grady, and no one dared challenge him. We had horses of both sexes coming and going over the years, and nothing seemed to make Leo sit up and take notice.

I suppose what's happening is not unlike the common story about folks who were in different cliques in high school, left for college and careers elsewhere, and reunited after maturity had taken hold, found a whole different person looking back at them. She'd been in love with someone else. He'd been on the outside looking in, perhaps trying not to let her know how he felt, as her boyfriend was the big horse on campus, star-football-player type. Suddenly everything is different. Grady is long gone, and Leo feels the need to be with Dolly, just hanging out side by side away from the maddening crowd. All night, that's what they do. They don't quite touch, but almost.

Come morning, the evil duchess (me) separates them. The first morning Leo yelled, tried to switch stalls with Dakota to be closer to his lady love, and generally made a nuisance of himself. I learned to bring him in first to forestall all the drama that had all the horses running in circles and peeing on each other. And during the day, Leo is sentenced to a separate turnout with his buddy, my mini, Duke. That's where he's been in the daytime for at least five years, and that's what works. Surprisingly, there are no histrionics involved in the separation. A couple of calls—like a newlywed husband touching base with his wife when he gets to work just to say he misses her—and then it's business as usual.

There's a lot to be said for love. Leo looks sharper and hunkier than he has in years. His renewed enthusiasm shows under saddle, though he's never been a slacker even at his most bored. Dolly is regal as always, but has visibly relaxed as the days have gone by. She is calm and cool and detached from any drama in the pasture, which has had a very quieting effect on the herd as a whole. That's another unexpected and very pleasant side effect of her return.

There's even more to be said for maturity. The two sweethearts are obviously bonded. Last night, in fact, Leo invited Dolly over to his paddock for a drink and dessert and would have managed to avoid turnout with the herd if I hadn't noticed his tail flicking behind the corner of the barn before I closed the gate. But there was no tantrum when I broke up their little lovefest and shoved them out the gate into the night. I predict that in another week, they'll be like an old married couple, and even the morning calls will stop. They'll just go through their days doing what they know they have to do, and at night they'll be side by side, sharing breath and grass and just loving their lives.

What more could anyone want?

CHAPTER 15

CURVES AHEAD

The phrase "there's a learning curve" is applied to pretty much everything these days, but reading the contexts of some applications makes me wonder how many people actually know what a learning curve is. Teachers of all sorts think they do, but much of the time they're really looking at a bell (or bell-shaped) curve and misidentifying it. Businesspeople generally have a better grip on it because it affects their bottom line, which is what business is all about. The average people on the street are more haphazard about the definition and nod knowingly when the phrase is thrown at them by someone speaking with some authority, like their dressage instructor. It's time we all got on the same page with this term.

First, I want to separate out the bell curve. They're both very curvy indeed, but the bell-shaped curve is a statistical model indicating that, in a perfect world, there will be a few really low-scorers on whatever scale we're using, a few really high ones, and the general population will fall in the middle in a curve that rises gently from the low and falls equally gently to the high end. The vast majority will cluster happily at the very top, where the ring would go were you to hang this bell on your cat.

The following image shows a bell-shaped curve. "Mean" means "average"—the total scores divided by the number of scores.

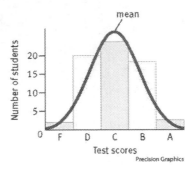

For example, if you have twenty novice dressage riders, one may be completely incapable of anything more advanced than learning how to laminate the card with the test on it and stick it under the pommel of her ill-fitted saddle. She would pin the bottom—zero—end of the bell on the left. Two may actually accomplish a sitting trot without needing orthopedic intervention above or beneath the saddle. Seven may accomplish a training level one test without being shown the gate for doing a sit-and-spin at X. Four may extend the canter without extending their health insurance to cover catastrophic injury. Three may get to level one, two to level two, and the last talented soul may make it all the way to shadbelly without an ER visit. Plot those numbers on a graph with the test levels across the horizontal and the number of riders on the vertical, and you'll get a rather sloppy bell shape, statistically satisfying if not attractive enough for framing.

A learning curve, on the other hand, isn't bell-shaped. It's more of a rise-plateau-decline. This is actually an Econ 101 concept. When a new business launches a new product, the first few efforts are very expensive and possibly deadly, with very little positive return. As the process is better "learned" on all sides of the business, consumers included, the effort is reduced and the profits increase. Eventually the peak performance level is reached, and since it can't get any better, it just sits there. Time goes by. Customers find a newer product, or the run on the one at hand is so great that the price of components rises, and lo, the curve tapers downward until the company gives up.

The following image shows a learning curve.

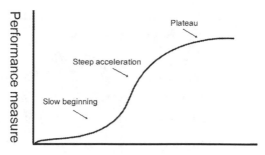

Number of trials or attempts at learning

It also applies to learning a new task, like dressage riding. At the beginning, there's a lot of energy expended, lots of money thrown at it, and very little performance payoff other than the sheer pleasure of throwing the word *dressage* into every conversation on every topic imaginable.

Boss: I need you to get this report out by close of business today, and hold all my calls while I'm in this meeting.

Newbie Dressage Queen (DQ): Okay. Just give me a minute to remove my dressage gloves that I'm still wearing since my dressage lesson last Thursday, and I'll use my *Inside Dressage Monthly* gimme pen to get right on that report.

As time goes by, the level of performance increases and the cost decreases, as it's averaged and prorated and hidden under "miscellaneous" in the check register. Eventually a peak of performance is reached. That may or may not have required additional outlay in the form of a much bigger horse and more equipment, but we'll pretend she's not going to go that way because she's smarter than that.

Once peak performance is reached, the expenses pretty much level off to a few new pairs of breeches, a saddle pad or two, a few entry fees, and the sole support of a dressage trainer for both rider and horse. These are the glory days, because from the top platform of the learning curve, everything looks rosy. But as time goes by, the thrill drops off with the reduced cost, performance may suffer, and family and friends may tire of endless afternoons at endless tests, limiting the thrill still further. In the end, our rider is left wondering if a new horse and a new direction might be just the ticket, and a new learning curve is born as breeches are replaced by jeans and a newbie reiner is born.

So for each hopeful rider, there is a spot on the bell curve and a learning curve to track the process of getting to that spot. You won't have to look hard to find either, but both might be best ignored if you don't want to consider the possibility that you should have stuck to needlepointing tea cozies. There are curves there too, but nobody cares.

CHAPTER 16

ROOM-ESCAPE GAME

I'm an addict. I'll bet that somewhere there's a twelve-step program for online computer Flash room-escape gaming addicts, though given the nature of the addiction, it would probably have to be more like a 213-step program in order to pique our interest. In any case, give me a quiet, rainy afternoon with nothing more pressing to do, and I'll spend it online escaping from fantasy rooms, apartments, basements, caves … somewhere I'd never go in real life.

An escape-the-room game works like this: The maker hides clues in the usually graphically austere floor plan of some alien space. The clues are obtained by solving puzzles. The puzzles are located by point-and-click searches around the environment. Click on the right spot on the statue by the door, and his tongue pops out with a six-tumbler combination lock attached. Figure out the combination, and the belly of the statue opens to reveal the screwdriver you'll need for some other puzzle.

The really easy games guide the player by turning the cursor into a finger or fish or star or something equally obvious when the right spot is located. I like those. The hard ones don't. In those games, one can click pixel-by-pixel for an hour and find nothing at all. I hate those. I generally don't even bother with the online cheat "walkthrough" on those because even cheating is too frustrating to be worth the time. I like reinforcement, instant gratification. Pat me on the head, and I'll follow you into the dungeon. Give me the battery that works the flash-light that shows me the combination to the door, and I'm yours forever!

This afternoon was hot and humid—far too yucky and fly-infested for a ride or a serious outdoor workout—so I sat at my desk clicking away. *Click!* Ah! A piece of pipe is hidden under the potted plant. Yay!

Eventually I solved the last puzzle, watched the graphically inter-esting landscape appear through the open door, and that's when the thought hit me that working with horses is the same thing. The horse has a bunch of trigger points hidden all over him, and it's up to the trainer to find them, click them in the right order, and maybe unlock a puzzle that can be easily solved with brilliance, logic, and lots of self-adulation.

The whole thing is a big, long, "if *a*, then *b*" argument. If I touch Pokey on the nose, then she will lower her head and close her eyes. I don't know why any more than I know why clicking the potted plant on my screen is likely to drop a piece of pipe into my inventory, but with Pokey, I know it's going to happen because it always does. In the game, the *why* isn't important. The player is merely guessing at what the programmer was thinking when he wrote the program. Both are human. One may have an obvious sense of humor. It's not impossible to sort out, because both start on an even playing field.

With the horse, it's a different game entirely. Finding the why behind the puzzle gives us the ability to replicate the behavior. No matter how much we'd like to think we can, we humans really can't *think horse*. We try. Heaven knows we do. But we are forever overlaying our faux horseness with our real humanity. We can't help it. The *why* is infinitely important, and totally obtuse. There are theories, but until horses learn to talk, they will remain just theories. But I wonder if it's possible to back away, take the "self" out of the equation, and play the game objectively, with better results.

What does the game designer want us to see that we're not seeing?

I'm going out on a limb when I say I believe that the horse really isn't in control of most of his reactions. He's the artistically designed game board. He's screen after screen of cool spots to click, but he isn't the one who put the puzzles there, so he can't really help with the solution.

It's all on us to bridge the unknown. There's no walkthrough available on any site anywhere. We create the puzzles by making demands for behaviors otherwise useless to the horse's daily existence, and we want them to be exhibited when we ask for them. But the hidden nature of the clues takes winning off the table. We're not in this to win; we're in it to survive. We just want that door to fling open while we're still young enough to see the pretty landscape outside and not immediately think of bug repellent and sunscreen.

And that is by no means a given.

Picturing my big-butted Appy, Dakota, I am truly at a loss as to where the puzzles might be hidden. I've been playing that particular game for more than seven years. When he arrived, he had one mode: sluggish. And it was with much flapping and urging and cajoling and cookie-feeding that he revealed two other modes: curious and running as fast as his chunky body would allow. To say that I clicked the right pixel and revealed the puzzle (which I then solved with tremendous flair) would be a total lie. I have no idea which of the multitude of cues I gave him finally moved him forward. That fact is obvious whenever I put another person on his back and try to instruct that person on what to do to make him move in any particular mode other than meander-transitioning-to-amble. I do know that the sight of a red fifty-gallon barrel excites him now that we've done some running around them. That was a new experience for him when I introduced it, and he spent a long time hanging over the fence, apparently mesmerized, as I did the pattern with Zip or Leo (or on foot, with Duke's little legs pumping hard beside mine). Once he caught on, it became a wondrous thing to him that he could run like that and make circles and get kudos for do-ing it. And pole bending! Let's just say his self-image has "Born to Run" emblazoned across the eight-by-ten glossies he imagines handing out to his fans. Sadly, they'll all be asleep before he gets to the finish line to hand out the pictures.

But there's no particular spot on his screen where I can swear that if I point and click there, he'll do something. Of all the horses I own or have ever owned, his game designer is the hardest to second-guess. I've found a spot on the top of his head that seems to click me a head-lowering, but it's subtle at best, not the obvious drop-to-his-chest that Zip does so willingly (and unexpectedly at times). We're doing clicker training now to try to make the puzzle a little clearer for both of us, but it's a slow go.

And I do mean for both of us, because the horse is just as anxious to solve the puzzle that is me. He would like nothing better, I'd guess, than to find a pixel to click that would get me to leave him alone or solve the cookie-feeding conundrum without having to input his own effort at some pointless task. He's at a disadvantage, though, because he doesn't own a computer. He hasn't played games and succeeded, so he has no template. Sucks to be him. We have to take our advantages where we find them.

As I type, the herd is grazing its way across the pasture. A few minutes ago, they were hovering around the trough, it being hot and humid as I mentioned. But as soon as the thunder started, off they wandered. Puzzle. On other days, thunder has brought them to the barnyard gate to be let into their fan-ventilated stalls to wait out the storm, but today they ignored my pleas and cookie-infused bargaining. There's one deeply hidden pixel that I will probably never find, the one that determines whether they seek shelter or throw themselves on Thor's mercy.

I believe this is one of those games that, online, I would have shut down to go have a cup of tea because my brain was fried. And so I will.

CHAPTER 17

THIS ABOVE ALL

I attended a retirement dinner the other day. I try not to do that, mostly because the honorees generally don't care much about older retirees showing up to eat the chicken and get sappy on cheap drinks. But this one marked the end of an era, as the last of the people I'd worked with prior to my own retirement were leaving to find new meaning in old lives. Somehow that seemed worthy of my attention and attendance.

Sadly, most of the attendees were my fellow retirees, not the current crop of workers, who one might imagine could possibly be saddened or elated or motivated by the imminent loss of a small cadre of their fellows. But, be that as it may, as so often happens at these affairs, I was asked repeatedly, "So … you still doing the horses?" That's exactly the way it's worded. Occasionally someone asks if I still "have" them, but "doing the horses" seems to be how my nonhorse friends see my life. And I assure them each that, yes, I'm still doing the horses, and I turn the conversation to what they themselves are currently "doing."

I find that no one "does" grandchildren, travel, motorcycling cross-country, or reading on the beach anymore. "Oh, me? I'm doing my neighborhood watch." Sounds obscene, doesn't it?

But linguistic quirks aside, I am always hard-pressed not to give the truest, most basic answer. I never say, "Of course I am. I have no other option." I don't say that because it sounds depressing, like a life sentence at a work camp for the feebleminded. It's not. It's the only way to describe how much a part of me "doing the horses" really is.

Of course there are days when I wish the horses would just go the hell ahead and do themselves for a while. I've been doing them for more than fifty years at this point. One would think they'd have learned some doing of their own by now, wouldn't one?

All of this thinking about doing got me twisted around to that scary place inside my horses' heads, and I realized that they might very well think that all these years, they've been doing me! Imagine it. Every morning they gather for breakfast. Maybe all that low rumbling and huffing and snorting is them discussing the day ahead.

Zip: Food. Food, food, food. It's daylight, and I'm not seeing food. *Rumble huff!*

Leo: Really? Is that all you ever think about? I think about getting brushed and fussed over. I'm a handsome guy, you know. It's nice to hear it from someone else occasionally. *Snort!*

Pokey: My butt hurts. I wish I could put my own goo on there. I hate having to wait and make sappy faces at the humans and all. If I had thumbs, I'd be a much happier camper. *Cough!*

Dakota: Love! Love, love, love, pet my head, snacks.

Leo: You're an idiot.

Dakota: *Sniff!*

Duke: Oh boy! Oh boy! Hi, you guys! Nice night out? Wish I could go out with you, but the human likes me in my stall when it's dark. I don't know why. Hi! Hi! Hi! Hi! The humans like me best. They throw you out to the scary dark because I'm the best.

Pokey: Geez! Shut up already. We see you. We're ignoring you. Grab a clue, why don't you?

Dolly: My stall. My stall! My hay. My water. Mine. Don't touch. I'll make the human bite you if you touch my stuff. I swear I will. You! Human! Zip is looking at me again!

Okay, that's probably nothing like what they're saying. I'm sure it's more a discussion of which part of the pasture still has grass and whether the deer need to be chased out or left alone and what that noise over by the arena fence might be … Really, I have no clue what they're thinking. But it's a safe bet I figure heavily into their agenda. Everyone is going to get fed. Everyone will be brushed. Someone is likely to be ridden. Everyone will have a nap. Everyone will go out again with fly hats on (which I'm sure are a bafflement to them). Everyone will line up again before dark and do the whole routine over. More humans might visit and feed cookies and coo and whimper. And all of it rests on me. I figure in almost every minute of their lives.

So maybe it's not me doing horses, but us doing each other. And in the end, I have the long end of the stick. I get all the fun of watching them watching me watching them, and I have thumbs, so I make a cup of tea or a martini and open the door and sit on the patio with my legs that bend the right way for chairs.

Yep, I'm still doing the horses.

But back to the retirement thing. I can't help but think that as horse people (persons of horse?) we might have a slightly different perspective on the gathering storm that is old age that follows so quickly on the heels of the rainbow that is the retirement dinner. Unless one is involved with animals, the life cycle is a little more abstract, I think. Sure, friends move to Arizona or a nursing home or a cemetery, but not every day, and not graphically right in our faces.

Animals—horses—are mortality on the hoof. Smaller animals even more so, as their lives flash by in a relative instant while we can usually keep the big critters alive long enough to watch them slowly fade, almost like our human friends. As horses age, they slow down in small ways. When horsemen age, it's with much anger and frustration, for one of the things that goes with aging is the growing inability to "do the horses." First we find help with the doing, and then we sit and watch the doing from the sidelines. Eventually even that stops, and we talk with other slowing-down horsemen about all the past days of doing. But though we might not be interested in showing up at a retirement dinner for a coworker, we are always interested in the goings-on in the herd. And we fight long and hard to keep doing horses.

One old friend regaled me with a litany of his aches and pains, ending with, "It's depressing when you hurt all over when you get up in the morning." Clearly he's never done horses. That ache-all-over starts with the first tumble from the saddle when you're still young enough to bounce, and it never ends. You can be six years old and know about the aching all over. It gets bigger and smaller, but it never ends. Yet we love it because it tests our mettle. Pain and anguish and loss and heartbreak and joy and excitement all come together in a big flash of what it means to really give in to living. Horses take us there.

And yes, we do horses.

Riding, tractoring, mowing, haying, farming ... the "ings" have it!

CHAPTER 18

Mow, Mowing, Mown!

When in the course of farm events, it becomes necessary to take a break from the fun stuff (like riding), a mower of some description is usually involved. Today was such a day. Despite the beautiful sunshine and the cool breeze, I found it necessary to forego the pleasure of a hack on some willing equine buddy and go tractoring instead. It was necessary because I couldn't see the horses over the weeds in the pasture.

For me, this isn't entirely a hardship. The vibration may set my teeth on edge, and my neck gets stiff from leaning over the side of the machine to get a close look at exactly where the outcrops of ledge rock are hiding. Hitting those with the flail mower's million little blades makes a horrible clanging noise that Cliff can apparently hear from work four miles away. One good *clang*, and there immediately follows a cell-phone text like "What did you hit this time?" I've given up making excuses and pretending that he hallucinated the sound because his low-fiber diet is taking a toll on his hearing. The only saving factor is that he hits more things than I do. And I don't have to replace those little cutting blades after he shatters them.

I've got my choice of machinery these days, which makes the job so much more fun. I can wrestle the mower onto my fave, four-wheel-drive, power-steering-augmented Mahindra. I don't often do that because it requires the removal of something called a "quick hitch," which, though quick, weighs as much as a full muck bucket.

Or I can plead with Cliff to put the mower on the International—his "baby," as he has entered his second childhood with both feet at the State Fair's tractor pull—which is not likely to happen. The International makes the job really fast, which is a good thing because getting on it requires a ladder and I have to stand up to disengage the clutch or use the brake. I don't want to have to do those things very often, so I'm delighted that the tractor is fast enough to cruise at low altitude and spin on a quarter (no tractor spins on a dime … sorry). Cliff, by the way, was kind enough to put running boards on this monster in the belief that I would be able to mount unassisted if he did so. Now I need a shorter ladder to get to the running boards. It's all a matter of perspective, I suppose. I don't drive the thing unsupervised anyway because … well … I haven't figured out how to start it.

There's also the old Ford 2000 in all its crusty blueness. That's the machine the mower has been attached to for a couple of years, leading to my ignoring the mowing jobs entirely and focusing my effort instead on working trade-offs to get Cliff to do them. Built about the time I graduated from high school, the old Ford is trusty, loud, and has no semblance of power steering. The steering wheel takes both hands and a lot of back muscle to make a turn tight enough to avoid going through the fence, and the PTO (that's "power take-off" for those of you who aren't tractor-tech savvy) has a scary feature that forces the user to rev up the engine, drop the mower, and then throw the monster in gear in what one can only hope is the correct direction, so that the mower will roar into life and not miss cutting the first four feet of whatever noxious growth is being attacked. This can be heart-stopping for the newbie. I know, believe me.

Today I chose the *new*-old Ford 2000. This is Cliff's most recent purchase (he always buys these things for *me*, by the way, using my height, slight build, or lack of experience as an excuse), and I have to admit that in the two years between the birth years of the *old*-old Ford 2000 and the *new*-old Ford 2000, technology moved forward with vigor. This beast looks exactly like the other one (to me, anyway), but it has power steering, and the mower can be gently coaxed into motion without the scary (and *loud*) burnout. He had me at power steering and no ladder required for mounting.

So instead of a lazy romp around the property on Dolly, whose turn it is in the four-horse rotation, I settled for a boring but effective effort to rid the pasture of inkberries before the horses turn purple. Big Blue and I ground a huge thistle to wet, green powder, took out a clutch of broadleaf, and prevented a new generation of weed trees from making the pasture fields smaller than I'd like them to be.

I'm not going to pretend it was fun, but there's a certain satisfaction in roaring up over a rise of ledge rock and actually seeing horses beyond the hill where shoulder-high weeds used to be. And the pretty photos I take and post on Facebook of my horses in the pasture are carefully timed for right after a mowing. June and August are weed-mowing. June and August are hay-mowing. For two months of the year, mowing is my life.

And, really, it's all for the horses' sake. It's not just my income that they absorb intact. Grass and hay and sunlight and water are what they need, and I aim to please. Of course, when I got the whole farm thing in my head and actually bought the New Jersey version of the fantasy of peaceful days, horses grazing in the green pasture, time to ride whenever I wanted, and no one to tell me what to do or when, I had no idea there was so much mowing involved. Or so much other stuff. Boarding out, one never really gets the whole picture. The barn owner or a spouse or partner does all the farm-y stuff when picky boarders aren't around to question modes and methods. To the boarder, it usually seems as if the land takes care of itself. All of the focus is on whether the stalls are clean and enough feed has been dumped into the feed bin and whether or not it's okay to put fancy brass nameplates on the stall doors. Inkberries only impinge on the boarder consciousness when the horses turn up purple from the knees down.

I learned about them when a fellow boarder got herself in an uproar and convinced all of us that evil teenagers had been firing at the horses at night with high-powered paintball guns. Since that barn owner wasn't into mowing, she had no clue that we were wrong and was as panicked as we were at the thought of armed vandals. It was another horse person commenting on her own horses' neatly stained white stockings and the inkberry bushes that were ripe in her pasture that helped us put it all together and stop calling the troopers to skulk around the place at night. Live and learn.

And you under-sixty-five youngsters, reading this and snickering and thinking that I still have plenty of time in the postmowing day for a ride, know that the thought has crossed my mind. It's still crossing, in fact. Crossings are much slower on this side of the hill. And there's math involved in the total energy available divided by the tasks to be accomplished and how many days of recovery might be expected. There are a lot of zeros on the downhill side.

So today I mowed, and tomorrow I'll ride horses without inkberry stains or thistles stuck to their noses. There won't always be a tomorrow, but this week there will be, and for right now, the path to happiness is neatly mowed.

CHAPTER 19

@# Ego

I wonder how long it will be before I learn that what makes my brain happy isn't necessarily what's going to work for the long haul. Sometimes I really surprise myself with my total lack of good sense.

This particular lapse can't be attributed to senility (though I do get a lot of mileage out of playing the age card), and it's not an effect of peer pressure. It's all me, all the way. I just can't quite figure out what I want to do when I grow up. In fact, I'm not at all sure I want to grow up. Being childish is so darned much fun!

There was a discussion going on online about creating images, and I don't mean the Photoshop variety. In particular, the commenters were cancer patients and survivors revealing their feelings about hair and body shape as related to the ravages of chemotherapy. I almost joined the chat, but to do so would have required me to create a login, and I'm fresh out. I have run out of cheeky/tasteful/meaningful words to use to separate myself from the hoi polloi.

I wanted to share that when I lost all my hair to the chemicals that saved me from the ovarian cancer that was my retirement gift from Mother Nature, I made a choice to buy every wig in the Paula Young catalog. Okay, not *every* wig. Some were just not my style. I bought many, probably twenty of them, because my decision was that I didn't want my disease to enter the room before me. Not embarrassment, not shame, not unease, just plain old egotism. I wanted people to look at

84

me, not my head. If there was going to be prejudging, I wanted it to be valid, based on my creepy taste in scarves or my mismatched socks, not my lack of hair and what it might or might not mean. And I wore those wigs with a sense of total abandon. I loved that I could look different every day if I wanted. I could look the way I felt. I wore them in private under my riding helmet, but that was self-defense. Until recently— when it was no longer necessary—I hadn't found a helmet that I could wear over my bald pate without leaving some scalp behind. And it was pure fun in a place where a lot of fun wasn't expected.

This isn't about cancer, though. And it's not about online discussions with total strangers or my inability to come up with new logins. It's about self-image. The question posed by the original blog post that sparked all the discussion was about how we want others to see us. That's where my point is lurking. I want others to see me the way I see myself, which is so inaccurate an image that it's laughable.

Yesterday I saddled up old Dakota for a quick ride and romp around the barrels in the riding ring. I wasn't really in the mood. He *really* wasn't in the mood. We managed a passable half hour, but there wasn't a whole lot of enthusiasm behind it. I give the big-butted App a lot of credit for putting up with my cowgirl fantasy on a hot afternoon when all he really wanted was to stand in his stall with the fan on, blowing the flies and sweat off his hide. Oh, there was a time when I actually did do some barrel racing and pole bending, but it was a very long time ago. Sixteen years ago, my barrel horse died, and with her my pretense of cowgirlhood.

But it makes me happy. Running around the old red barrels in my too-small riding ring or weaving through the red-white-and-blue poles I bought on a whim last summer makes me think I can do anything I want. That makes my brain happy, but eventually it's going to do my poor body in. So will popping Leo or Zip or Dolly or even beleaguered Dakota over the fancy PVC jumps I bought at about the same time that the poles came in the mail. I do not feel compelled to stick to one fantasy at a time. I'm a serial fantasizer. My "combined training" course involves running around a barrel, over a crossrail, around another barrel, over another crossrail, and then doing a dressage pattern and taking a short trail ride. No moss grows on my fantasy world.

The problem with all this is that my youngest horse is seventeen. The other three are in their twenties. I'm a woman of (*ahem!*) a certain age. Put all that on a spreadsheet, and the bottom line isn't really healthy for (wo)man or beast.

Dakota really tried to let me down easy. He could have been irritating or refused to do what I asked. He was his usual accommodating self, if you don't count the part where he tried hard not to go anywhere near the mounting block. I had to drag his thousand pounds of reticence by main force, and that's never a good way to begin a happy ride. He didn't buck or fuss, just planted his feet. And I looked him in the eye and said, "I promise I'll make it short … really."

He warmed to the job after a few minutes, and we managed a partial effort minus the crossrails, which I figured would elicit an "Oh, no, you don't!" and a ground smack I wanted to avoid. And the trail ride was shorter than I would have liked, as I got tired of spinning around in the middle of the lawn in a battle of wills. I settled for what I could get without bloodshed and then turned the old guy out in the barnyard, where he grazed happily while I dragged the ring footing to make it all good for my next retrospective visit to the land of abilities past. Then we both had a cookie and called it a day.

My self-image could probably use some updated firmware. I need to go to Me 3.0 if I'm going to survive this horse life. But to do that means letting everyone else see me as I really am, and that's just not in the plan. Typing that, I realize that actually, no one but me is looking. As Oprah once said on TV, "You'd stop worrying about what other people think of you if you knew how seldom they do." So my only audience is me, my self-designer is me, and the only one fighting this update is … me!

Food for thought, indeed, and I'll get right on that after I drag the riding ring and set up the jumps and poles and barrels again for my next combined pretense training session.

CHAPTER 20

Ω

FLATTENING THE HORSE WORLD

If you haven't already read Thomas L. Friedman's books about economics and the way the world is getting flatter by the day, that's okay. You should read them. That's homework for everyone who lives on the planet. For the time being, suffice it to say that Friedman is a genius I only wish I were related to.

The flat-world thing died with Columbus, right? Isn't that what you're thinking? Well, you're wrong. The world got really round for a couple of hundred years, which made astronomers and astronauts very happy, but now it's gotten flat again, and it's all because of the Internet and the World Wide Web monster.

What Friedman means by a flat world is that communication of ideas is now completely global, as is the transfer of ready cash, and the horse world is certainly feeling all of that. Anything anyone wants to know or make known is available worldwide in the blink of an eye, even if it's untrue, stupid, foolish, badly timed, ugly, or simply off-center. For horses, this has meant that more horses are moving around the country and the world at a faster pace than ever before, and misinformation is moving along with them.

The first round of crazy back in the mid-1990s involved spreading the gospel of the horse far and wide. Breeders found a much wider market for their animals, horse lovers were able to fling their horse love around like rose petals on a bridal carpet, and the idea that anyone who wants a horse can and should own one became a mantra. It's not hard to see the circular nature of that: more buyers, more money, more breeding, more press, and more buyers … and on and on.

The second round came in the form of the quick transfer of money into and out of institutions where money likes to live, and from those institutions the market crash of 2008 was set free to ravage the land. The ability of the world to send and receive stuff and ideas overwhelmed humans' ability to think through to the end of the process. Greed travels at quantum speeds; thought, not so much. Horse owners, like everyone else, got zapped; horses (especially those without satellite feeds in their stalls) were left behind.

But that wasn't the end. As horses got left behind, the unwanted horse got a lot of global online press, and out of *that* flatness grew a mountain of effort to make him more wanted. In the positive column, the list of rescue organizations aimed at the problem grew like Topsy. In the negative column, the list of frauds and fake charities grew even faster, and more money flew around the globe in the coy wink of an eye. Nigeria spawned a national entity in the form of scammers who thought horse owners were easy pickings, and they were right. I first saw this when my daughter was selling the tack she made for plastic model horses on eBay and I took over the business for a short period while she was away at college.

Customer: Please it is your wonderful mare a boy horse or a girl horse?

Me: It's a plastic horse.

Customer: Praise to *God* I find a horse for to be ridden by my beautiful daughter. Is you horse safe for childs?

Me: It's a plastic horse. It's not alive. There's no riding involved. Do you want to buy the horse?

Customer: I need know how tall is it, and if so, I will send to you a *money order* for 10 thousands dollars US today.

Me: It's seven inches tall. How tall is your daughter? And the price is $5.00 US.

Customer: *Most excellent friend,* you will receive a *money order* for $10 dollar US thousands today, and please so kindly send back the remainder after cost and shipping. *Bless you!*

Me: Here's the deal: I won't sell you this horse because it is not ready to ride, but I've got a pair of garden weasels I can let you have cheap instead.

Long story short, he wouldn't give me my price for the garden weasels, and my offspring and I are cursed for eternity. In a round world, that curse would probably never have reached me.

There is a great deal of chatter these days about globalization and how to prevent it. It would seem that many people missed the memo that it's been here since at least 1992, when I first mouse-clicked into the new era. By 2000 it was possible for a horse person in New Jersey (*moi*) to guest-write a horse column in Massachusetts without anyone thinking it strange. By 2001 terrorists were using Twitter to set up bombing matches. Now we have Wiki everything, so anyone who wants to can share information, valid or invalid, with the world with no prerequisite of actual knowledge, education, or common sense, and seekers are burdened with the problem of sorting the wheat from the endless supply of chaff. The only consolation is that the wheat-beating is going on around the world around the clock, so no one needs to feel singled out.

In the horse world, this flattening has had its benefits. I now own saddles made in a country I've never seen, purchased at a price I would never have expected, and with free global shipping thrown in as incentive. In fact, most of the time I'm completely unaware of the country of origin of the stuff in my barn. I checked while I was writing this and found that of the three "twenty-inch tether rings" I bought from a stateside catalog, two were made in China and one in Pakistan. And I found that out by using my smartphone to scan the barcode on the tags. Talk about flat! My phone knows the code for countries I one day hope to visit, and I can't remember the zip code for my brother's house.

Of course, the most obvious flattening in the horse world has come in the area of horse valuation. Naturally I got my license as an equine appraiser the day the market crashed. My life is full of such irony, so it didn't surprise me for a minute. I've watched the values of horses—what people are actually willing to pay for them, not the price the hopeful sellers have put on their heads—plummet. It's still possible to recoup what you paid for your beloved equine buddy whose beloved-ness has dimmed since your mortgage was foreclosed on, but it's harder now. The flattening has come about because shoppers, who used to physically drive from local sale barn to local breeder as directed by local newspaper ads, never before had a worldwide market for comparison. If the buyer lived in an area where particular types of horses were selling at premium prices, he had no way of knowing that just a few miles away, the same horses were going at fire-sale rates.

Now, thanks to the Internet, there are no secrets. If I tell you my gelding out of Stripper Two by Pacemaker is worth $20,000, I'd better have a pile of blue ribbons and proof that he's a moneymaker, because you can go online and in no time find out that Stripper Two was knock-kneed and Pacemaker was retired because he killed fourteen people. No lies, no harm, no foul.

Like it or not, we're a flattening world, and I, for one, am taking advantage of it. I'm wearing imported socks under my American-made boots as I ride in my Australian saddle, and my horse sports a British-made bridle. And I'm going to do my best not to delude myself into believing that the papers in a folder in my desk make my horses worth a dime more than someone (preferably not a Nigerian scammer) is willing to pay for them.

Can you see them? Mommy ears found them in seconds.

CHAPTER 21

MOMMY EARS AND HORSE TALES

The herd was a little sluggish yesterday when I called them for dinner. When that happens, I have to walk out into the pastures to get their attention. Like a bunch of kids, if they're busy with their own activities, my calling them in from playtime frequently elicits a *Huh? What? Were your talking to me?* response. Sometimes it's more like, *In a minute! Sheesh!* In either case, it's aerobic for me and not so much for them.

The way my pastures lay out on the property, it's impossible to see from one into another, and the one above is invisible from the ones below. In two of them, the horses have carved out their own loafing areas under the trees. Finding them isn't just a matter of a quick glance into a field; it's hide-and-seek, with a little CSI adventure sometimes thrown in. I can find Pinky and re-create his latest epic adventure by looking for the white hairs clumped on trees and rocks along his route.

So as I walked yesterday, I realized that it's been years since I actually had to cover every inch of the land to locate the hiding equines. I noticed with surprise that I was completely tuned in to sounds around me, and that a single hoof-stomp by a fly-ridden horse would immediately tell me where they were hiding. I could even tell which horse was stomping because they each have a unique approach, from Zip's casual "I really shouldn't need to stomp at flies, as handsome as I am" to Dolly's frenzied *Kick, kick, kick ... bang!* You don't want to be near Dolly when she's after a fly on her belly, because her ire knows no species boundaries and her hind legs are like jackhammers.

Listening, I could hear a small *tippity-tap* and knew that was one of the many fawns lurking around my place. It sounded as if this one was in the "rock pile"—a small treed rise in the middle of the front pastures—slowly checking for edibles around the edges of the stony mound. Birds, a squirrel, the *shush* of my young cat, Maxine, slicing across the grass barely touching ground in a lunge for some vermin she'd targeted ... all noted and accounted for. And in the distance, a quiet snort.

Ah! The horses were in the back field. Case closed.

Stopping where I was (no point in walking farther than necessary), I did the usual, cupping my hands and calling out the litany, "Zip! Pokey! Pinky! Dolly! Dakota! *Dinner!*" And I waited. In a minute or so, I heard the first hoofbeats and could tell that I only had three respondents slowly trotting toward me—Zip, Pokey, and Dolly, in that order. Sure enough, a heartbeat later they emerged from the trees and came over the small rise. I commented as they passed that it would have been polite to tell the other two that dinner was on, but they were otherwise engaged.

I waited another beat and then called again, "Dakota! Pinky! Move it!" Then I turned and followed the first three. From the barn, Duke and Leo put a loud exclamation point on my last call, and I heard the unmistakable sound of Dakota flying along the rocky path behind me. I didn't bother listening for Pinky. His *clop, clip, clop, clump* would follow shortly, as soon as he noticed he was alone and had made one shout-out to his buds to confirm his suspicion that he'd been abandoned once again.

I removed fly masks from the herd members closest to the gate (the command "hat" is something I taught them along the way to make my life easier, as they turn their heads to me and lower them for fly-hat collection or installation) and opened the gate so they could march in order into their stalls. I love how they do that! I listened for the sound of Zip making a stop in someone else's room, but there was none, so I yelled, "Good boy, Zip!" And once everyone was situated, I listened for another minute for the sounds of each of the herd members eating dinner. There's always a chance that I'd missed that Leo had pooped in his feed bucket during morning naps—it happens—and I can tell by the way he rattles the bucket as he tries to eat around the manure that I need to grab it and do a replay on his feeding. And Pinky is so darned old that I always have half an ear for any shortage of chewing noises coming from his stall.

With everyone settled, I hied myself to the house to make dinner, and when I walked through the door, it struck me that while I'd been engaged in a reverie about how much like the original Native Americans I must be to be able to put my ear to the clouds and hear horses, I'd really been doing nothing more (nor less) than using the mommy ears I earned more than thirty years ago.

If you're a parent, you know what I'm talking about. Mommy ears: that extra-sensitive hearing that can discriminate between a child doing homework and a napping recalcitrant. It's the ear set that I used to freak out my daughter by yelling up the stairs things like, "We do *not* use the second dresser drawer as a ladder, young lady! And pick up the laundry you just dumped on the floor. I'm not washing it again!" Once or twice she asked me how I knew, and I just shrugged. I preferred to operate swathed in an air of mystery, like a ninja.

It was one of my high school students who dubbed the phenomenon mommy ears. I was sitting at my desk inputting grades into the computer, and without looking up, I yelled across the room, "Billy, knock it off and get back to work!" Billy, startled, said, "You've got your mommy ears on! I hate when my mother does that. How can you tell it's me?" I just smiled. Mystery, thy name is … me.

However we come by our supersensitive hearing and ability to locate the source of a sound from somewhere out of sight, most of us have it. Some of us are numb to it. Cliff, for instance, can identify a hairy engine noise from a mile away, but he'll make four guesses at what that sound is coming from somewhere in the same room he's sitting in, and in the end he'll still be wrong. My daughter has two toddlers, so hers is even more finely honed than mine is, and it amuses me no end to hear her tag "Dillon just dove over the arm of the couch again" to a sound I didn't even hear.

It's my humble opinion that we would be a lot better off if we spent more time in the quiet focusing on those sounds emanating from the world around us and less filling our airspace with mechanically produced noise. TV comes to mind, and our own endless voices. But maybe that's just me and what I need to do. I, for one, find the constant attack of sound on my ears to be confounding and annoying, and while it hasn't seriously dulled my mommy ears, it certainly has made me crankier than necessary.

And on that note, it's time for me to go listen for the horses again.

CHAPTER 22

THE HEIGHT OF MATURITY

Kids have it easy. Put a little helmet and a pair of rubber boots on a five-year-old, and people will come out of the woodwork to give the tot a "leg up" on whatever willing equine is standing nearby. Let him fall off in the woods, and I swear gnomes will appear, stack themselves, and see to it that he's remounted and back on the trail. I didn't start that young so I missed that part, but I've watched the scene play out countless times.

When I started at thirteen, my instructors were all about giving us a real leg up. No picking up our cute little selves and tossing us onto the horse's back with a smile. It was the hop-hop-jump mount that was favored. I was still light and easy to toss, but probably not especially cute. I've got my school pictures from that era to attest to my total lack of adorableness. But there was never a mounting block around. I had never heard the term. If there was no one around to bounce me into the saddle, I had to drop a stirrup, scale the horse's side, and then crank the leather back up before he moved from walk to trot to flat-out I-know-you-can't-stick-up-there hand gallop. If nothing else, it was really good for the balance. In the fifties, we all had an independent seat, or we landed on the ground. We could dress and undress from a mounted position if necessary. No coddling was allowed, and as I noted earlier, parents tried not to watch, as it was really bad for the blood pressure.

When I was in my twenties, mounting blocks appeared, but they weren't popular among the under-thirty crowd. We tough buggers thought mounting from the ground on the fly was the way to go. Since I was apparently a girl, finding a boy around to give me a boost was rarely an issue. My cuteness level had soared in reverse proportion to my scrawniness. Once curves appeared, so did guys willing to give a girl a hand—in every possible way.

By my thirties I was starting to appreciate large rocks and tree stumps along the trail, as pee stops increased dramatically postpregnancy. Mounting a bareback horse meant climbing the fence and leaping aboard, but it was a matter of style, not necessity. It was intolerably cool to slide my limberness across a wide back, particularly in full view of whatever audience might be available. By thirty-seven, with my daughter firmly in her own saddle, riding out on the trail bareback was just the very utmost *in* thing to do.

My forties came along, and things got more interesting. I've never kept a record, so I don't know how many unplanned dismounts it takes to create arthritis in places where I didn't know I had joints, but it's a number I've reached. In fact, I probably created the joints as well. Mounting blocks suddenly appeared on my horizon, the little two-step model made of plastic that one could move around with one hand while being dragged across the arena by the horse attached to the other. Those were truly a boon, those little stools. There was no research yet on the stress mounting from the ground puts on the horse's back, so I had nothing to back up my fetish other than a bad back. That was plenty good enough.

By forty-eight, I was still climbing fences to jump on a bareback horse and still racing on the reclaimed railbeds, but mounting from a step, stool, bucket, or block of some sort was no longer just a matter of choice. I lucked into a boarding farm where actual wooden mounting platforms nearly as high as the horse's back had replaced the little two-step plastic block, and I was golden! I didn't need an excuse. Everyone who was anyone used the fancy-pants platform.

When I turned fifty, I literally bought the farm. Things went briefly downhill as tractoring and heavy lifting added crunching to the creaking. For a while I had to schedule rides on my tallest horse, big Zipper, for days when I hadn't been stacking hay bales, because I needed to be able to lift my leg high enough to at least reach the stirrup from the top of those two-step blocks. I bought a second block, so I had one in the riding ring and one outside the gate for those trail rides on horses who weren't so good at the mounted open-the-gate trick.

By the time I was nearing sixty, the most exciting experience of the year was the discovery of a three-step block hidden away under a shelf at Tractor Supply. I couldn't have been more pleased! I crammed that sucker into the backseat of my Audi, risking dents and scratches in the leather but bound for glory, as I'd finally be able to ride a horse over fifteen hands high even on a bad day.

I now own two of the three-steppers, and one of the old two-step blocks is situated outside the farthest pasture gate along my riding trail, where it keeps me from having to walk all the way back to the barn to remount when I've had to heed nature's (or gravity's) call. As I worked the other day on Zip's mounting-block skills (he has a tendency to wander his butt just far enough away to require me to leap a bit), I recognized that my age has been reflected quite clearly in the height of my mounting aids.

In light of that discovery, I've put in an order with Cliff for a four-step-with-handrails affair. By the time he builds it, I'll need it.

CHAPTER 23

Ω

ENDNOTE

No, it's not really the end. Not for me, anyway, and probably not for you, but certainly for this book. We horse folks are a hardy breed who are unlikely to give up our fetish until forced by circumstances. When Connie Reeves, cowgirl par excellence, died at the age of 101 after a fall from her horse, I think we all puffed up our chests just a bit (though dragging our boobs out of our belts was a trial for some of us) and thought, *I'm going to do that! I'm going to ride until I'm so old I'll just die in the saddle one day.* I know I thought that.

Reality has a way of undermining our fantasies, but it never hurts to have a goal. I may not be riding at 101, or ninety, or even seventy-five. I don't know. What I do know is that the horses don't make me feel old. Age does that all by itself. Being horse bound is my most valuable affliction. The horses keep me moving forward, putting one foot in front of the other, ignoring aches and pains, and looking forward to the alarm every morning because each day is different from the last. I admit that my free time is filled more often with trips to the theater than with horse shows. I wasn't all that fond of competition, so that's no loss. I still appreciate looking at pretty horses and watching good riders, but it's not my focus any longer.

No, my focus now is on the moment. This moment, which is all I have, has to be the best it can be. And the next, and the next, and all the moments lining up ahead of me, all have to be the best they can be.

I wish I'd known that when I was younger. It would have been nice to appreciate every moment instead of letting so many rush by in a dither of drama and craziness, none of which I can clearly remember but all of which seemed vital at the time. I would have filled more of them, I think, with breathing in the smell and feeling the heartbeat of whichever horse was in my life at that moment. And I would have been kinder to the people as well. Less competitive and more helpful would have been a better approach. Mostly I would have crammed in a few more moments whenever I could have. The day when three of us fellow boarders set up our own pretend show in the riding ring at a boarding farm is such a warm memory for me that I wish I'd done that more often.

Now I try my best to actually *be* with the horses, not just stand around near them. I don't mind if Leo, the aging quarter horse, just doesn't feel like being ridden and would rather cuddle. That's a good way to spend time. And if Dolly wants to do nothing but practice the same dressage test over and over because it's the one she's memorized, that's okay too. There's nothing to be gained from doing things that serve a faulty or fraudulent purpose, so being real is what I'm after.

Or so I shout from the lofty perch that is my current postretirement life. Hindsight isn't 20/20; it's a falsehood created from whole cloth as part of our fiction.

If there's one thing I could pass on to my daughter, it would be the ability to stop and just focus on the moment. Unfortunately, that seems to be something that we don't learn until we get old. So instead I will wish for her—and for all the young riders out there—a headlong rush into the full-out joy that is life with horses. Go forth and be crazy! It's a wonderful way to go. You can make up a story to cover your folly later when you're old, like me.

About the Author

Joanne M. Friedman is owner/operator of Gallant Hope Farm in New Jersey. Over the sixteen years since she bought the farm, it has morphed from a training/boarding/lesson barn into a private farm, where hay and sanity and humor are produced in equal quantity. Prior to adopting the farm life, Joanne spent twenty-five years teaching high school special education. In an earlier life, she graduated from Clark University with a BA in psychology and from the University of Hartford with an MEd in special education. She has been an equestrian for more than fifty years and a freelance writer for twenty of those. She has written over 350 articles on horses for various websites and magazines and numerous articles on other topics for financial and psychological newsletters and websites. She is the author of *It's a Horse's Life! (Advice and Observations for the Humans Who Choose to Share It)*, *Horses in the Yard (and Other Equestrian Dilemmas)*, and *Horses Happen! (A Survival Guide for First-Time Horse Owners)*. Friedman is the author of the blog *Horses in the Yard* at http://joannemfriedman.blogspot.com/.